HOLY
HUNCHES

HOLY
HUNCHES

responding to the
promptings of God

bruce main

BakerBooks
Grand Rapids, Michigan

Published by Baker Books
a division of Baker Publishing Group
P.O. Box 6287, Grand Rapids, MI 49516-6287
www.bakerbooks.com

Printed in the United States of America

Library of Congress Cataloging-in-Publication Data
Main, Bruce.
    Holy hunches : responding to the promptings of God / Bruce Main.
        p.   cm.
    Includes bibliographical references.
    ISBN 10: 0-8010-6803-7 (pbk.)
    ISBN 978-0-8010-6803-4 (pbk.)
    1. Christian life. I. Title.
BV4501.3.M246 2007
248.4—dc22   2007001668

To Rob Prestowitz, Colin McArtney, Wayman Crosby, Bruce Robinson—for faithfully embracing those who have a hunch to serve our city's children. Bless you.

Contents

ACKNOWLEDGMENTS

To the thousands of college-age interns who have tithed a summer or a year of their lives to serve the children and teens of Camden, Wilmington, Toronto, Vancouver—thank you.

To the faithful volunteers of UrbanPromise Ministries, you give in so many creative and wonderful ways—thank you.

To the thousands of donors who faithfully send gifts each month, enriching the lives of children and teens you will never know—thank you.

To my friend and editor, Paul Keating, for never tiring of good works and good words—thank you.

This world is a better place because of you all.

INTRODUCTION

A NEW WAY OF UNDERSTANDING

How do you want to spend your life? We all know you can ruin it. But what is more important to recognize is that you can sleep through it.

Dean Brackley

I've noticed an interesting phenomena—a pattern, a theme.

As director of an urban youth ministry, I receive, probably as often as once a week, a phone call, a letter, an email, or a visit from a hardworking professional. The occupations of these professionals vary—lawyer, doctor, journalist, financial manager, small business owner, university student . . . a vocational potpourri.

And their theological and political views are as varied as their identities: Lutherans, Pentecostals, Catholics, or Baptists, Republicans or Democrats.

Or try their geography or ethnicity: African-Americans, Korean-Americans, Euro-Americans, Canadians. And socioeconomic background doesn't seem to matter either.

But they all have one thing in common: their Christian faith.

So why are these Christians trying to connect with a ministry that helps children in Camden, New Jersey, which has been deemed America's most dangerous city? Is it simply their Christian faith that motivates their calls and emails? I don't think so. If that were the case, I would be inundated with calls 24/7.

It appears there is a deeper reality taking place in the lives of the callers and emailers.

Sure, they may be interested in serving in different capacities, whether it be painting a wall, mentoring a kid, answering phones, tutoring a failing teenager, teaching a class, pulling weeds, cutting grass. But the one constant is that each wants to engage in an act of service because of something happening in their lives now.

But what is going on in their lives now? What motivates their steps toward action? Is it the connection between the teachings of Jesus and Christian service? Is it some affinity with the Old Testament's accounts of Micah's and Amos's commitment to justice? An inspiring magazine article or book? A good sermon?

After all the introductions and explanations on the phone, the prospective volunteer might say that they heard someone from our organization speak the previous Sunday. I'll often ask, "I'm curious. Out of last Sunday's congregation of at least eight hundred, you are the only one responding. Everyone heard the same sermon, sang the same hymns, heard the same cantata and pastoral prayer. How come *you* decided to call?"

After a little hesitation, they might respond, "Well, um, I don't quite know how to respond to your question. I just *felt* something."

"You *felt* something?"

"I know it sounds a little vague," they quickly add, "but I'm not exactly sure how to put it into words. How about it was just a . . . hunch. Yeah, maybe that's the best way to describe it. I just had a hunch that I should call."

The response always fascinates me. Out of a truly diverse group of people, an impressive cross-section of professions and denominations, the callers use similar language to describe a particular phenomena. And they use the word *hunch*. "I just had a hunch." Coincidental?

After years of undergraduate and graduate studies in theology, seminary, and a doctorate in ministry, I have to admit that I have never heard the term *hunch* used in any of my academic settings. Well, sure, I did doze off occasionally in a lecture—systematic theology after lunch was tough, and keeping the eyelids open during Hebrew class at eight a.m. was almost impossible—but I still don't think this word *hunch* was ever proposed as something worthy of academic reflection.

Yes, "calling" was discussed. So were spiritual gifts— discerning our gifts, taking an inventory of our spiritual gifts, or exercising our gifts. And of course, I read all kinds of tomes on the Holy Spirit and vocation. But hunches? I can just hear the learned professor of hermeneutics: "That's hardly a word for a seminarian!"

Reflecting on the theme of calling, vocational choices, spiritual gifts, or the Holy Spirit certainly is critical. But my ministry experience informs me that there might be another language—new words—to help Christians understand the phenomena that takes place when we feel compelled to move in a God-inspired direction. Perhaps theologically heavy words like *calling* and *vocation* need to move aside and give room to more earthy words like *hunch* or *nudge*.

Why is it important to look for new words to help understand the Spirit's work in our lives? Let me first say that a vast number of Christians do not work in jobs where they feel a deep sense of calling. Statistics on job satisfaction suggest that a significant portion of our population feels little connection between their job and a sense of spiritual fulfillment. And, when pushed, most would contend that their jobs do not allow them to exercise their spiritual gifts at all. Living a called life is a distant reality for most people.

Consequently, we go to church and hear sermons about Abraham's call, the apostle Paul's roadside conversion, and the disciples leaving their jobs to follow Jesus. We hear dramatic stories about missionaries who follow God's call to a remote part of the world. We leave the sanctuary inspired. Yes, but we also leave feeling a little disconnected, knowing that we're never likely to live in a leper colony, smuggle Bibles into a communist country, or head up some medical outpost in northern India. We're not that adventuresome. Sure, we may understand the language of a "called life," but we may not resonate with the concept because of the realities of our lives—commitments to aging parents, family medical care, monetary need, debt . . .

So that may be why I keep hearing the word *hunch*. People are looking for ways to live spiritually spontaneous lives in the midst of careers in which they might not feel a true sense of calling. And this is exciting, because a vibrant spiritual life should not be reserved only for those who find a deep sense of spiritual fulfillment in their work lives. God-inspired hunches can happen to ordinary people who do ordinary things like raising families and paying mortgages.

Regardless of our place in life, hunches come to those who take the time to open themselves to the Spirit of God. Hunches are what prompt us to put our faith into action, despite the job we hold, the stage of our career, our ethnicity, our age, or the demands and realities of our circumstances. Hunches, *holy* hunches, ultimately nudge us toward expressing God's heart and intentions in our world at any time in any place. Hunches don't necessarily demand a career change, or call us to sell our homes and move to a developing country. Not that a hunch can't or won't do that. But hunches, holy hunches, inevitably move us to live more faithfully and authentically in the moment and place in which we find ourselves.

Oh, and by the way, I confess that I approach the issue of a hunch-inspired life with some trepidation and hesitation. Because of the subjectivity of the hunch word and its experiential implications, the potential for harm and misuse is a strong possibility. There are hunches that lead to the expression of God's witness in the world. But there are hunches that have the potential to produce hurt and destruction.

My hope is that this book will help people make distinctions—the distinction between divine hunches that are holy, wonderful, life-giving, and those hunches that lead in an opposite direction.

As Mother Teresa of Calcutta once said, "I am but a pencil in the hand of God." As we open ourselves to the nudges of God, my prayer is simple: may the exciting adventure of our individual experiences leave behind a remarkable and beautiful portrait of a life that expressed the exquisite presence of God. If we are faithful to and excited by our hunches, our holy hunches, I believe this will happen.

PART ONE ◀■

➡ WHY HOLY HUNCHES?

⇨ 1

A HUNCH AND NITROGEN-BASED ICE CREAM

We are not lords, but instruments in the hand of the
Lord of history.

Dietrich Bonhoeffer

I had just finished the last bite of a massive and delicious
wedge of apple pie, which had capped off a wonderful meal
and an intriguing conversation. "Could you use a chemist
in your ministry?" my dinner host, Dr. Daryl Cox, asked.
He was a handsome, middle-aged professor who wore bi-
focals halfway down his nose. I was caught off guard by
the intensity of his question. A chemist? Of course, lots of
people have volunteered at our inner-city youth programs

and schools, helping to paint walls, scrub toilets, tutor kids. But a chemist? How could I use the talents of the eminent doctor of chemistry in our youth programs?

I was on a recruiting trip to a small Midwest college on this particular trip, and a few faculty had taken me out to a local diner on the final night. All that week I had shared with an audience of college students about how our staff and volunteers work in America's poorest cities, providing after-school programs, sports leagues, summer camps, and alternative educational opportunities. (Our school in Camden, New Jersey, which meets in a cramped, converted row home, is an alternative high school that has become an oasis for teens who have dropped out of their schools or have performed well below their academic potential.) Now I was just enjoying the moment to unwind and fantasize about that second piece of pie.

But Dr. Cox persisted. "Do your youth have an interest in understanding the elementary principles of chemistry? And if so, could you use me for a week?" Daryl Cox, PhD, head of his chemistry department, was serious.

"Well, um . . . I'm sure they must," I stammered, not knowing exactly how to politely dampen his enthusiasm. "I'll be sure to check with my staff." I guessed he would forget about us when he returned to grading midterm exams. After all, wasn't Camden, New Jersey, a world away from Oklahoma City?

However, when I returned to my New Jersey office the next day, there was an email from Daryl Cox. He wanted to make sure I was following up on his offer to serve. His enthusiasm had not waned at all. I called our modest high school to talk to our director.

After a few minutes of brainstorming and "oh wowing" and laughing about what to do now, our principal and I decided that she just might be able to block out a week of class time for Dr. Cox to teach an introductory chemistry course to our seniors and juniors. When? The last week of the school year. Why? "Well, the kids don't do much that week anyway," Principal Rogers reasoned. "Are you sure he wants to do this?"

After all, a chemistry professor who is comfortable teaching college students just might find inner-city high school kids who struggle academically to be a real test. And chemistry during the last week of school? Not a chance. The kids would either eat him alive or be so bored they would skip the week. I felt certain Dr. Daryl Cox was going to be in way over his head.

But, on May 29, 2004, Daryl Cox rented a U-Haul van and loaded it with Bunsen burners, laptop computers, beakers, and an array of chemicals. For him it was a sixteen-hour sojourn into the unknown. Like Abraham of old, the good doctor was leaving for a place "he knew not."

And oddly enough, instead of traveling 850 miles directly to Camden, New Jersey, Dr. Cox decided to swing by Greenville, Illinois, to pick up his college roommate from 30 years ago, who also happened to be a chemist. Who also had a PhD. Who also happened to teach college students. And whose name was, well, you guessed it . . . Darrel. So, there were Darrel and Daryl cruising down the Pennsylvania turnpike in a white rental van.[1]

After they arrived late Sunday afternoon, I showed them the living room of our staff house, apologized, and said, "Well, uh, here's your lab." I was certain it was just a little different from their gleaming, state-of-the-art facilities back at their respective colleges. We were as grassroots as it got—primitive, even.

I returned two hours later. "Wow, you really made this place look like something professional. I'm impressed."

Impressed? Yes. But I was worried. The professors were used to captive audiences—pre-med college students who take notes and pass tests so they can beef up their GPAs for grad school applications. Our kids, on the other hand, doubted they would ever go to college. Our kids were the ones the local public schools had written off. Daryl and Darrel were about to have the test of their lives.

The first day of chemistry class, the students made nitrogen-based ice cream, which led to an instant party. One student, Shamar, met me at the door with a mouth full of white creamy stuff and screamed, "Our science experiment!" Dr. Cox and Dr. Ilers had successfully captivated their imaginations while introducing them to the basic concepts of chemistry.

Surely, by day two, the attention of our teens will wane, I thought.

But on day two the students were measuring relative levels of CO_2 in cans of Coke and Pepsi. "Shake the cans and try to determine which soda has more gas." Of course, shaking cans of soda and spraying it over the parking lot was pretty cool stuff.

By day three the classroom was percolating with chemical concoctions, and graphs were appearing on computer screens. And by day four, the students were hooked. While kids in other schools around our town were cutting classes and getting ready for their proms, our students were captivated by the elementary concepts of chemistry.

By the end of the week, the students were sharing with their newfound friend and mentor their fears about college life. "We'd love to go, but we don't have the money." "No one in our family has ever gone to college." Daryl listened, counseled, and talked to those young people about their fears, how they could prepare for college, and how they could access scholarships. "You can do this," he said with conviction.

Besides having their minds exposed to the wonders of chemistry and its connections with everyday life, our kids witnessed how Daryl and Darrel integrated their Christian faith into their lives and vocation on a daily basis. As a director of a program, I cannot put a price on this kind of witness, this kind of testimony. Their faith was real. Our kids just knew it, felt it.

A few years have passed, and, yes indeed, a number of those curious young people have gone on to college, two into pre-med programs. In a community that sees fewer than 10 percent of its high school graduates go on to a four-year university, our students are living proof of what can happen when God's people get together and share their lives and gifts. Some of our students still keep in contact with our chemists.

When I think back to that wonderful five-day chemistry adventure, I remember how it all began at that diner in Oklahoma City. I think back to a man whose heart began to stir. Dr. Cox had a prompting to step out of his comfort zone, to surrender his gifts to the intentions of God.

⇧

And it all began with a hunch. Some might call it a divine nudge, an inspiration, a calling, or a revelation. But I like to call it a hunch . . . a holy hunch. These hunches happen during the course of a normal day—in the shower, at the breakfast table, at work, during a class. Our hunches often prompt us to actions that reflect the heart of God in the world. Our hunches challenge us to ask questions, make phone calls, write letters, and engage in spontaneous acts of generosity. Like Dr. Cox's hunch, they challenge us to explore a new possibility. They call us to move beyond the routine.

Hunches are hard to explain. I have yet to find the term listed in some weighty theological dictionary. I don't think John Calvin or Karl Barth, Augustine or Luther ever devoted a page of their luminous commentaries to the idea of hunches. But just because these theological heavyweights of church history never wrestled to define a holy hunch does not mean that the word is not significant and does not need our reflection. Or, just because there is not a clear, logical definition for a word doesn't mean the word is irrelevant. Most of us have an intuitive sense of what someone means when they use the word *hunch*. We may not have the ability to clearly put it into words, but I guarantee we connect with the word in an experiential way. Using *holy* as an adjective simply means that the hunch comes from God, or moves us toward the things of God, rather than from some other source that might lead us in another direction.

After all, as Christians, we pray, we worship, we read the Scriptures in an effort to open our hearts and minds to the creative movement of God's spirit. We go through those exercises not simply to show our devotion to God but to open our heart, to prepare our mind for God to speak—for God to give us a hunch. And I believe that when Christians open themselves to the Spirit, they have hunches all the time.

The bigger question centers on what to do when they come.

My experience tells me that our hunches are too often repressed, stifled, or denied. The great enemies of our hunches —fear, practicality, arrogance, insecurity, and laziness—rise up and shackle us from acting on these promptings. Disapproving voices from friends, family members, husbands and wives can override what we know to be true. The negative tapes in our heads, the admonitions from our childhood to be serious or to act "appropriately," switch on and squelch that still, small voice of God.

Yet when we do respond to our holy hunches, God's presence in the world is often released in remarkable ways. When we respond to our holy hunches, our faith is stretched and deepened. Lives will be changed. Dreams will be ignited. Ministries will be birthed. God's love will be acted out in the world. And inner-city teens will be turned on to the wonders of chemistry.

⇨ 2

Opening Doors for Ordinary Miracles

The truth is, anyone who believes in me will do the
same works I have done, and even greater works.

Jesus (John 14:12)

Miracles are overrated.

Now, don't be offended. Let me explain.

When most of us think of miracles, we envision people
dramatically cured from a fatal disease, or overcoming a life-
crippling addiction, or being resuscitated from a near-death
experience. If you're anything like me, you probably never
imagine yourself performing a wonder such as lengthening
a leg with just a wave of the hand, fixing a root canal with
a touch of your finger, or removing a cataract with a mere

blink and nod. As of today, I have not been invited to a party because of my ability to turn water into wine. Performing miracles is not what I do. I'm just an ordinary guy who interacts with ordinary people.

But, thinking of miracles only in terms of the supernatural is a problem for many of us, and when we think that way we immediately disqualify ourselves from participating with God in something rather . . . well . . . miraculous. If spectacular healings, walking on water, or parting oceans is our functioning model of miracles, we dismiss ourselves from the process of the miraculous. This is why I feel that rethinking our ideas about miracles and seeing the interconnected relationship with our holy hunches is critical. Believe that the miraculous is closely connected to your life. Then you can open yourself to a whole new dimension of Christian faith.

Let's revisit our example from chapter 1.

University professor Dr. Daryl Cox taught chemistry to inner-city teenagers in a three-bedroom row home. That is close to a modern-day miracle for me. Not convinced? Perhaps you embrace a more C. S. Lewis–like definition of the miraculous—a definition which contends that miracles are an act that violates the natural laws of the universe; they're an in-breaking of the divine into the created order, causing something out of the ordinary to happen.

But reconsider my PhD friend for a minute. He and his friend spent a week in what has been deemed America's most dangerous city—at their own expense, and on their own vacation time—to open the minds of young people to the wonders of chemistry and the possibility of a university education. That may not be considered a miracle in your book, but it is certainly close in mine. After all, how many college professors have spent time teaching impoverished, inner-city kids in a dilapidated three-bedroom row home? Very few. That probability likely ranks with winning a lottery or being struck by lightning twice. University professors visiting poor, urban communities to teach chemistry to academically challenged youth is certainly a very rare occurrence.

But if you are still not convinced that such things are a miracle, stay with me a little longer. When I asked Dr. Cox if his trip to Camden was a miracle, he blushed in a self-deprecating way and humbly replied, "No." Rather, he saw his visit simply as an expression of his Christian commitment, as an extension of what it means to live out faith in the world. Dr. Cox was caught up in the ordinariness of driving 1,200 miles, filling his gas tank at his own expense, drinking paper cups of stale coffee, and preparing lesson plans. And that is why most of us miss the point when it comes to experiencing the miraculous. The ordinariness of our daily lives too often blinds us from seeing the bigger picture—the miraculous presence of God working *through* our ordinariness.

Consider the following: what if Dante, who attended Dr. Cox's weeklong chemistry classes, goes to a university because of the inspiration of Dr. Cox? The patience of the doctor, coupled with his passion for chemistry, infected Dante with a kind of self-confidence that he never experienced before. Instead of taking the minimum-wage job at the local nursing home, which his mother wanted him to take, Dante filled out his college application form and got accepted. In a city where fewer than 10 percent of kids go to a four-year university, this feat verges on the remarkable. Perhaps not a miracle in your eyes, but for me we're getting closer.

For the sake of my argument, let's say that Dante does go to college, takes a keen interest in biological research, and gets a scholarship for graduate school. The odds of a kid from my neighborhood making it to graduate school are probably about one in ten thousand. Further, Dante finishes graduate school, is invited to intern at a biotech company, and develops a vaccine for some worldwide epidemic that can save thousands of people from death and suffering. A far-fetched story? Perhaps. But it happens.

Take the story one step further. Dante, who was initially inspired by Dr. Cox, and who helps develop a vaccine at the biotech company, finds that his company is not very altruistic and instead has a board of directors that is totally driven by the bottom line. Their interest is in making money, and they look at the new vaccine as an opportunity on which to capitalize. But Dante, who was deeply impacted by the sacrificial faith of Dr. Cox and by now has developed his own faith, becomes the moral voice for the company and challenges the company to use the newfound revenue to provide discounted drugs for poor people. And the company board of directors, enamored by the faith and commitment of the young man, decides to embrace his broader vision and take a portion of their profits and product and invest it back into impoverished communities. Besides being a great story—the kind you might make a TV special about—it is getting close to the miraculous. And it just may happen.

Perhaps I have not convinced you that Dr. Cox's teaching in Camden is a miracle, but I think you would agree that the miraculous outcome of this student's journey could never have happened without the faithful professor responding to a hunch. Dr. Cox's willingness to act opened a door for the possibility of a miracle to occur. Without his initial act of faith and his response to his hunch, the chain of events leading toward a miracle would never have started. When Dr. Cox got in a U-Haul on a May afternoon to begin his cross-country trek, he set in motion a series of events that could lead to one more miracle in our world.

Throughout the Gospel narratives there are many miracles: people are healed, crowds are fed, water is turned to wine, and dead folk come alive. Certainly Jesus' array of miracles impresses us and continues to inspire sermons, books, and endless theological discussions.

But one has to ask: how many of these miracles would Jesus have performed had there not been a human being responding to some kind of hunch? In many miracle stories we see Jesus responding to a person who initiated a movement toward him. People who experienced the healing touch of Jesus were usually acting on the hunch that an encounter might lead to something miraculous. It's interesting; Jesus' miracles were generally precipitated by a human—not a divine—initiative.

Take the healing of Bartimaeus, the blind beggar, that is vividly described in Mark 10:46–52. Bartimaeus, who had sat by the roadside day after day, cried out as Jesus passed. Despite the admonishment of the crowd telling him to hush, Bartimaeus persisted. Bartimaeus certainly was acting on a hunch—a hunch telling him that if he could get Jesus' attention, something special might happen. Instead of repressing the hunch, or just cowering, he acted. He yelled over and over, "Son of David, have mercy on me!" Jesus responded to Bartimaeus acting on his hunch. Which at least raises the question: would there have been a miracle that day had Bartimaeus remained silent? If Bartimaeus had listened to the crowd and dismissed the hunch, would Jesus have stopped? If Bartimaeus passively sat by the side of the road would he have experienced a healing? Hmmm. Not likely. The miracle happened because Bartimaeus opened a door for it to happen.

The feeding of five thousand people described in the sixth chapter of the Gospel of John is another example. Isn't this story really about a boy who had a hunch—a hunch suggesting that Jesus might be able to use the miniscule gift of a few fish and five meager barley loaves? I don't know about you, but I would have been embarrassed and afraid to step forward with such a paltry offering. I'm sure there were people in the crowd that day who thought, *If I bring my lunch rolls and cheese to Jesus, he'll laugh at me.* Yet some voice deep down inside the boy believed that if he could get his lunch into the hands of Jesus, *something* might happen. This miraculous event happened because a boy followed his hunch and offered his food.

Or take the healing of the paralytic in the fifth chapter of Luke, another example of a miracle that took place because of human initiative. Does it not begin with four friends who had a hunch? A few men believed that getting their good friend to Jesus might create an opportunity for a miraculous healing to take place. So, one day the four friends take a day off work and meet for an early morning latte at the cafe to talk strategy about how they could get their friend halfway across town for an audience with Jesus. "If Jesus just touches him, that'll be enough . . . but you know there'll be a huge crowd—there always is. Can we get near?" And sure enough, just as they thought, when they got to the house where Jesus was talking and healing, there was a huge crowd. But, the men acted on their hunch—they climbed up to the flat roof, took off some of the tiles, and lowered their friend through the roof!

The story turns out to be a wonderful example of Jesus' compassion and healing power. But would the paralytic have experienced healing if his buddies had not acted on their hunch? Would the paralyzed man have experienced healing had his friends not taken the second step and lowered him through the roof? I don't think so. The miracle took place because a group of friends followed their hunch—it was what opened the door for the miraculous to occur.

I could list many more examples throughout the Gospels that illustrate the connection between the miraculous and what I call a holy hunch. Throughout Scripture we see the pattern. Miracles are not always simply an act of God. The miraculous is not always just a divine interruption of daily life that comes out of nowhere. Rather, there is often a human dimension to the miracles we read about in the Bible—both Old and New Testament. It seems that God's modus operandi is to involve human beings in the process of the miraculous. The faithful acts of ordinary people create a space where the miraculous occurs, like how a farmer tills the soil and plants the seed in preparation for a bountiful harvest. And as each of us is called so a miraculous activity can take place, we need to be open to holy hunches in our daily adventure of faith.

Let's now look at another example illustrating the connection between a hunch and a miracle.

⇨ 3

Hunches Working Together

> Every word, every action, every effort of our lives has a
> ripple effect. Because of us, others will either do more
> or do less to co-create this world. "Every action of our
> lives," Edwin Hubble Chaplin wrote, "touches on some
> chord that will vibrate in eternity." What do you want
> to hear played there on your account?
>
> Joan Chittister

It was 6:42 in the evening.

Brent Liebman, one of our talented staff workers, was scheduled for a seven o'clock appointment in my office.

But at that moment Brent was driving down South 4th Street when he saw eleven-year-old Margie Rodriguez standing outside her row home. Her family and most of the block's residents were crowded together on the sidewalk.

Brent pulled over, even though he was running late and Margie was not part of his plan right then. He was supposed to be bringing four girls, Shonda, Abby, Alyse, and Peaches, to meet a couple of reporters from ABC News. The reporters were looking for a poignant story—a human interest story about good kids trying to navigate a difficult neighborhood.

But when Brent saw Margie, he sensed something was wrong; her house was taped off much like a TV crime scene with yellow plastic ribbons. A black and white police car ominously blinked and swirled its warning lights. Brent thought the worst. Margie ran up to him and said with tearful alarm, "They're gonna bulldoze our house, Mr. Brent."

"How come?"

"Don't know . . . but they're not even letting us back in the house to get our stuff."

"That's not right. How come they're not letting you all back in?"

"We tried, Mr. Brent, we tried. But the police said they got their orders. Now we got nothin'."

That's when Brent had a hunch. *Scrap the interview with the other girls.* Margie was the one who needed to see the reporters, not those girls who'd been scheduled. In Brent's mind those New York people would get a great story. This was a family Brent knew; he'd watched the kids grow up. His hunch overruled rationality.

When Brent and Margie walked into my office, the reporter and the two other girls I had recruited were more than surprised. I had promised ABC that there would be a group of girls; now here was just one. So much for impressing ABC with my ability to keep a commitment. I'd have a word with Brent about following directions. Didn't he know it's not every day we get featured on ABC?

"I decided to bring Margie instead of the others," my program director said with a sheepish grin, as though we would all be delighted and impressed with his creativity. "Something happened to Margie's family this afternoon. So I thought the reporters would want to know. It just felt right."

Felt right? I was unaware that Brent was a budding journalist. What about the plan? I didn't want to make a scene in front of our reporters, but I wanted to ask—no, yell—"Brent, does one just abort the mission because something *felt right?*"

"I hope you're right on this one, Brent," I whispered.

The interview with Margie got started but wandered from one inconsequential topic to the next: school, books, boys, hobbies. I sensed the reporter's frustration; she wasn't quite getting *the* story. This kid wasn't connecting with her intention. The reporter glanced at her watch. It was time to get on the road, time for the exasperating traffic up the New Jersey Turnpike into Manhattan.

Brent furtively whispered in Margie's ear, "Tell her about your house."

"They're gonna bulldoze my house," Margie blurted with a somber look. "They're not even lettin' us back in to get our clothes. Nothin'. They's just givin' us one night at a hotel."

Margie and the reporter sat in a moment of suspended silence as if the reporter needed to regroup.

"How's that make you feel, Margie?"

The child blinked. No one had ever asked her how she felt. People in her world just didn't take the time to ask. "I feel afraid," the usually street-tough little girl said as she stared at the carpet.

"Why afraid?"

"Everybody'll laugh at us," she said tentatively as a film of tears edged over her chestnut brown eyes.

"Why would people laugh, Margie?"

"Because people always laugh at homeless families." You could feel the hurt as the reporter reached for Margie's hand and lightly held it. A dramatic shift in their relationship occurred—it was no longer a detached correspondent from the big city, not just another jaded reporter. She pulled out her business card, slid it across to Margie, and assured her she could call for free . . . any time. "I always return my phone calls," she said warmly. They hugged, and we all headed to the parking lot for our cars.

I knew our reporter friend needed to get home, and even without traffic it would be at least an hour and a half drive . . . maybe two. She'd get home after eleven.

As we headed toward the parking lot for our respective vehicles, impulsive Brent pulled Margie aside and whispered something and directed her toward the reporter.

"Could you come to my house?" Margie asked shyly.

I was sure that at the end of a fourteen-hour day, the reporter's thoughts were already heading north on the Turnpike and imagining a chilled glass of Chablis, a reclining chair, and a carton of Chinese takeout she'd pick up on her way.

But apparently something within the correspondent's being nudged her to make a counterintuitive decision. I'll call it a hunch, a holy interruption that was triggered by the tentative, whispered request of a child.

She turned the key in the ignition, and the engine leaped into action. "Sure, Margie, I'll come to your house. Show me the way."

The Power of Credentials

When little Margie and her entourage arrived at the 700 block of South 4th, the police were still there. Now more residents on the block had been forbidden to enter their homes. Bulldozers were on their way in the next few days, and the police obviously were indifferent to the families that had been displaced. "Hey, don't blame me. We're just following instructions," they complained. It just didn't matter that the landlord of the properties had failed to tell the tenants that he had received a letter announcing the condemnation of his properties and the dates of demolition. Certainly none of this had been passed on to Margie's family. Why would anyone leave a family of seven stranded with no place to live?

But now the Rodriguez family had an ABC reporter who was holding the hand of a little girl from these row homes. "I'm from ABC News," the reporter said to the young police officer.

"What's ABC News doing here?"

"I'm doing a story on this little girl, Margie, who lives in this house. It'll be aired on ABC—you know, to a national audience. I'm wondering if you'd want to make a few comments about why you won't let the family go into their home to get their belongings."

The novice police officer, obviously put on a job that required little experience, was momentarily befuddled. He stammered, "Well, um, I guess I'll call my supervisor. Just give me a minute, ma'am."

Surprise, surprise. Within a few minutes, Margie and her family were packing their possessions. Their housing problem had not been solved, but at least they would have their clothing and a few of their treasured possessions.

And that was just the start.

Within the hour, the one-night voucher for a local hotel had miraculously turned into two weeks, buying a little time to provide the family with some other temporary housing.

With ABC News watching the situation, the city politicians and social workers would now be accountable to a much broader audience. The earlier indifference to the plight of this struggling family now would not go unnoticed or undocumented. The reporter and her camera crew were there until the story played out and had a positive ending. It's amazing how our attitudes can change when we know we are being watched.

Converging Hunches

The next day when I called the reporter at ABC to thank her for going the extra mile at the end of her long day (confronting the police, getting the family back into a home, using her clout to influence a few decision-makers), she interrupted: "You know, Bruce, every morning I begin my day with a little Franciscan prayer.

> Lord, make me an instrument of your peace.
> Where there is hatred, let me sow love;
> Where there is injury, pardon;
> Where there is doubt, faith;
> Where there is despair, hope;
> Where there is darkness, light;
> Where there is sadness, joy.

O Divine Master,
grant that I may not so much seek to be con-
  soled as to console;
to be understood as to understand;
to be loved as to love;
For it is in giving that we receive,
it is in pardoning that we are pardoned,
it is in dying that we are born to eternal life.[2]

And, you know what? I'm continually astounded by what happens. God uses me in some really wonderful and surprising ways."

We talked for awhile longer—about Margie, about faith, about how she follows a story. After hanging up I realized something special had occurred. Some people might interpret it as just another random series of events. Luck. Fate. Coincidence. But I knew there was a thread connecting the past day's events. It was as if there were some kind of interconnectedness between the spontaneous decision of Brent and the reporter that led to a result that reflected the intentions of God.

Brent and the reporter acted on their hunches. Those two people took a risk by breaking away from their own agendas. Consequently, when a holy hunch reverberated through them, nudging them toward an act of justice, both Brent and the reporter were willing to become God's chosen vessel. They fulfilled God's vision and plan for Margie and her family. They had become the common ingredients that resulted in a glorious banquet; the reporter and Brent were needed to complete God's mission.

For me, this story vividly demonstrates the interrelatedness of our hunches. It shows how individuals, acting on their hunches, can converge and bring about some startling, wonderful results. But the story also reminds me of how God's witness in the world can be thwarted by a person not willing to follow through on their hunch—the chain, so to speak, is broken. Would the plight of Margie's family have been discovered had it not been for Brent's sensitivity and courage to go in an uncharted direction? I doubt it. Despite the unpleasant circumstance, would little Margie and her family know that God still cared had it not been for the reporter's listening to her inner voice? Perhaps not.

I wonder how often God's witnesses of love and peace in the world are not fully realized because holy hunches are not pursued. How different the world would be if God's children were consistently faithful to the hunches they sense.

We've Never Seen Anything Like This!

Some men came, bringing to him a paralytic, carried by four of them. Since they could not get him to Jesus because of the crowd, they made an opening in the roof above Jesus and, after digging through it, lowered the mat the paralyzed man was lying on. When Jesus saw their faith, he said to the paralytic, "Son, your sins are forgiven."

Mark 2:3–5

The culmination of the story of Jesus healing the paraplegic in Mark 2 describes a group of people standing around, rubbing their eyes, praising God, and saying, "We've never seen anything like this!" It was spectacularly new for this group of eye-rubbing onlookers. A paraplegic jumping off his bed and skipping merrily down the street at the command of a local religious teacher was not a common sight. This was, in the words of Eugene Peterson's Gospel translation, *The Message,* "incredulous."

But witnessing an incredulous event should always beg the question: how did this happen? Why? Many of us get caught in the "wow" of the moment. We are so dazzled with the outcome of the miracle that we fail to see the smaller, seemingly ordinary choices and decisions that led up to the miracle. Like the crowd that witnessed the healing of the paraplegic, we rub our eyes and say, "Wow, we've never seen this before!" In the dazzle it's easy to miss the significance of the ordinary.

In Mark's reporting, four friends converged in an act of faith and charity. It was an act that had an incredulous result—the healing of their friend. Besides the healing, and important to the story, are the lives of the four people who worked together. It was not the faith of one person that began the chain of events leading toward the miracle. There were four people coming together around what I would call a common hunch. It was a mutual hunch that compelled each of the men to believe that Jesus just might be able to do something for their friend. It was a hunch that motivated them to do more than sit around lamenting the condition of their friend.

Besides the lesson surrounding the paraplegic's healing, I find that the stretcher used by the men to transport their friend is a powerful and galvanizing symbol in this Gospel narrative. Underscored by Jesus' affirmation about the faith of the paraplegic's four friends (Mark 2:5, "when Jesus saw their faith"), the stretcher became the instrument with which those men could act out their hunch. Just four men, each grabbing a handle of the stretcher, got their friend to a place where he could *possibly* experience the healing touch of Jesus. Four people moving together. Four people responding, in congruence, to their hunch. If one dropped a handle, if one man backed out or couldn't go on, would the mission move forward? Would the miracle take place? It would seem not.

Listen to my fictional dialogue of the four men prior to their excursion of faith that day. (My literalist friends may have problems with my dramatic conjecturing, but some kind of unrecorded conversation took place on that day as those friends were thinking about taking their crippled friend to Jesus.) It was, let's say, Samuel who initiated the plan.

> "Hey, Marc, I heard there's this teacher who's supposed to heal people. And he's in town. And I hate seeing our brother in his crippled condition. Remember when we were kids? He was the one who outran us all."
>
> "Funny you should mention that, Sam," Marc said. "I was just thinking about him too. And this might be our only chance to get Paulus back on his feet. Let's do it."
>
> "Should we get Peter to help?"
>
> "Nah. Old Pietro wouldn't do it," Marc lamented. "He doesn't believe in this kind of stuff."
>
> "Yeah, I know, but we gotta have two other guys. We can't drag Paulus across town ourselves; he's a dead weight, and my back's not in great shape. I must've sprained it the other day."
>
> Marc's eyes lit up. "I've got the perfect guys—the twins! They'll probably think the idea's a little crazy, but they're usually willing to take a risk."

"Perfect!" Samuel shouted and gave Marcus one of his great flashing smiles and a high five. "But I'd better talk to my boss and see if I can get the day off. Nah, I'll just take a sick day, otherwise he'll think I am out of my mind, hauling some sick guy around."

None of us will ever know for sure what conversation took place before these four friends embarked on their journey to bring a paraplegic to Jesus. But we do know that the healing would not have taken place had these friends not acted *together*. Their collective willingness to obey their hunches placed their friend before the feet of Jesus. The convergence of dedicated friends following their hunches, each grabbing hold of the handle of a stretcher, created an opportunity for something spectacular to take place. There is interconnectedness between these individual acts. The story illustrates the power of what can happen when a group of individuals is faithful to a hunch.

"Stand up. Take your mat. Go home," said the masterful voice.

Converging Lines of Faithfulness

James Fowler, a developmental theorist, provides an interesting metaphor when it comes to understanding how God moves through a chain of people who are acting faithfully on their holy hunches. Fowler looked at a historical event such as the civil rights movement. He observed how God moved through numerous people in that movement, through people who were acting on hunches that would begin to lead our country toward justice and racial reconciliation. God moved through various human beings as though they were links in a chain to bring about a massive social change.

Fowler claims that people often identify a leader like Martin Luther King Jr. as the instrument that God used to expose the evils of racism. Fowler does not negate the importance of a man like King, but he believes that God's presence in that movement was linked to the faithfulness and courage of thousands of others who lived before King.

> We see the persons who stood behind them [King] for generations back. We see the influence of teachers and mentors brought together with them at crucial moments for some element of preparation and development that would be decisive in an as yet unanticipated future.[3]

What Fowler underscores is that King's emergence and success as a dynamic leader were directly linked to the lives of other faithful people—people who spoke words of truth to King, people who modeled courage, and people who for years had been faithfully acting on hunches, preparing a platform for his ministry. According to Fowler, there was a convergence of many lives in the life of Dr. King. Fowler writes:

> Such factors as these begin to make visible to us how the divine praxis draws together long lines of convergent faithfulness in order to bring about redemptive transformation in the midst of peoples and of history. And they lead us to reflect how faithfulness in our vocations may contribute—far beyond any set of connections we can now see or imagine.[4]

Or picture it this way. Imagine a roaring river—it has energy, force, and the awesome ability to change a landscape. But go upstream and you will see that the river divides into smaller rivers. As you trace some of the smaller rivers you realize that they also divide and become yet smaller. The roaring river is really a collection of smaller streams. The cascading river you first visualized is simply the final expression of hundreds and hundreds of tributaries that in concert have mounted in force and power. Thus the expressions of the miraculous in our daily lives are merely the result of many people being faithful to their holy hunches.

Fowler encourages Christians to view themselves as tributaries. As each person walks in faithfulness, seeking God's witness, love, grace, compassion, and justice in the world, our efforts combine with others on the same journey. Our converging lines of faithfulness—dynamic expressions of God's presence and movement—become visible in the world. Our lives and actions are connected to bigger movements of God in the world. Likewise when we fail to walk faithfully—or fail to respond to our hunches—a tributary is blocked and fails to connect with the other tributaries of faithfulness. Do we know how our lack of faithfulness will impact the future movements of God? Do we know how many lives will indirectly or directly be impacted because we are selfish, fearful, impeded by our rationality or our disobedience? Our choices, our actions make a difference to others—and to God.

Without the hunch of my young staff worker Brent Liebman, the reporter would never have met Margie. Without the reporter, the police officer would never have felt inclined to let the family gather their possessions or treat them with dignity and humanity. Without the reporter and Brent acting together, one of God's frightened little children may not have been reminded that God's eye is always on her.

PART TWO ←

→ OBSTACLES OF
HOLY HUNCHES

⇨ 4

Overcoming Inferiority

You made [people] a little lower than the heavenly
beings and crowned [them] with glory and honor.

Psalm 8:5

My wife and I decided to skip the final Sunday morning session of a three-day Urban Church Conference, opting for a
few moments of quiet conversation before our long drive
home. The session probably would have been invigorat-
ing, but with the demands of our careers and raising three
preteens, Pam and I decided to do something we seldom
do: breakfast together . . . alone.

The restaurant was delightfully empty and quiet. With no
competition at the buffet, we decided to forgo our diets and
indulge in extra bacon, biscuits, and grits. Oh, the Southern-

ers really know how to cook, and we certainly didn't want to see any of that delicious food go to waste.

As is our style, however, within a few minutes of enjoying the great regional food, we found ourselves in a discussion about what high school our fourteen-year-old son should attend. He was to begin the ninth grade in a few months, and there were a number of factors to consider: location, quality, finances. Not surprisingly, I had my opinion (the right one) as to where he should attend. Pam had hers. And so between the sips of coffee and forkfuls of hash browns, we tried to move in the direction of an amicable decision. Nice try. After thirty minutes of back and forth, we found ourselves at loggerheads—we were diametrically opposed on what we thought would be best for our son.

At that moment, the bishop who presided at the conference the night before unobtrusively slipped through the doors and sat in a secluded back corner. He also had given the sermon, the one we'd skipped, at the morning session of the conference. I figured he had excused himself early, just to have something to eat before leaving for the airport.

Now, I must tell you that my wife is not a person who lets an opportunity pass. She excused herself and walked over to the bishop. She shook his hand, motioned to our table, and gestured him to follow. I was afraid to look. "What seems to be the problem?" he began after greeting me and sitting.

I confess that sharing my personal business with a bishop is not something I do. If I were a Roman Catholic, I might have drawn a connection with the confessional experience, but being a Baptist gave me no comfortable point of reference to share intimate details with a person of ecclesiastical power. I hesitated. I knew that this man of the cloth wanted to enjoy one of the few quiet moments of his week. But now his solitude was interrupted by a heated discussion between two parents whom he had never met. I could only imagine his private prayer: "Come on, Lord, I'm just trying to savor a plate of eggs! Can't I have a little peace and quiet?"

In my embarrassment, though, I said a quick good morning and blurted, "Well, um, my wife and I have a difference of opinion as to where our son should go to high school." Saying it out loud made our argument seem even more trivial. "She wants him to go to one school. I want him to go to another."

For the next ten minutes he listened to both sides of the discussion, asked a few questions, and then offered his opinion. Wouldn't you know, he sided with my wife! And who's going to argue with a bishop? Oh, it was going to be a long, quiet ride home.

Just as he was getting up to leave and go back to a cold breakfast, my wife grabbed him by the arm. "Do you mind if we pray for you?"

The bishop looked startled. I'm sure people seldom made this kind of offer to him. After all, he was the ecclesiastical pooh-bah—the one always praying for and blessing other people, officiating at weddings, reading last rites, facilitating denominational meetings. Now my wife wanted to pray for him, right there in the restaurant! What would be next?

"Well, uh, sure," he stuttered, "That would be nice."

Pam stood and placed her hand on his shoulder. She motioned for me to do the same. So, there in the restaurant of the Best Western Hotel, my wife prayed for the bishop.

Now, one must understand a little about Pamela. One of my close friends calls her a "force of nature." Others have called her spontaneous, even impulsive. I know her as a person who is led by her heart—someone who gives little credence to protocol. She just says and does what she feels in the moment.

When the last amen was muttered, I opened my eyes to glimpse a tear rolling down the cheek of the bishop just as he wiped it away with his index finger. To my surprise he stood there transfixed—there was no movement toward his cold eggs and grits.

"You know," he began, "this morning in the general session I asked everybody to find someone in the audience and sit next to them and pray together." He paused in an effort to regain his composure. "After I made the announcement from the pulpit, I said my own little prayer to God. I asked God to send someone to pray with me. I waited. No one stepped forward. Alone, I stood at the front of the auditorium and watched everyone praying for each other." He took a deep breath and then looked at my wife. "I find it amazing, perhaps even miraculous, that in my coming to breakfast I would find someone who wanted to pray for me. Thank you . . . thank you."

He turned toward his table and started to walk away, then stopped, turned, and added, "You know, I was beginning to feel like God had abandoned me. Thanks for reminding me that God is still there, listening to my prayers." And with that, he returned to his table.

When we sat back down, my wife gave me a smile. Hah! *She* had the bishop's blessing regarding our son's future, and *she* had once again allowed herself to be used by God to bolster the faith of another believer.

"Why did you pray for him?" I asked with a degree of curiosity. "I mean, what possessed you to pray for the bishop?"

"I guess I just sensed he needed prayer. You know," she said with a mischievous twinkle in her eye, "I just had a hunch."

I have to confess that even if I had been given the hunch to pray for the bishop, I probably would not have acted on it. My mind would have immediately released ten reasons not to pray—you know, like, "Bishops don't need prayer," or "Isn't it a little presumptuous to make such an offer to a bishop? After all, who am I? What if he laughs? Snubs me? Corrects my theology?" I would have rationalized the hunch into repression and willingly surrendered to the social norms of our culture and church hierarchy. To pray for a bishop, in a restaurant, no less, takes a degree of chutzpah. It takes a willingness to disregard the social barriers that guide our thoughts and govern our actions—those barriers that tell us that one human being is more spiritual than another, or a person's vocation gives them an elevated status. For me, praying for a bishop is like offering a physician medical advice or correcting a literature professor's grammar. One just doesn't do that! There are certain boundaries of authority that one should respect . . . aren't there?

Fortunately, Pam does not live by those boundaries. Pam follows her hunches. And because she does not allow herself to be silenced by the unspoken social codes of our society or by a sense of personal inferiority, a bishop was blessed and his faith was encouraged. Like the biblical woman with the hemorrhage, the one who momentarily suspended her position as a social outcast and publicly approached Jesus, Pam overstepped what many would deem appropriate and reached out to a brother, a bishop, in need. God did the rest.

Overcoming Inferiority

> A large crowd followed and pressed around [Jesus]. And a woman was there who had been subject to bleeding for twelve years. She had suffered a great deal under the care of many doctors and had spent all she had, yet instead of getting better she grew worse. When she heard about Jesus, she came up behind him in the crowd and touched his cloak, because she thought, "If I just touch his clothes, I will be healed." Immediately her bleeding stopped and she felt in her body that she was freed from her suffering.
>
> Mark 5:24–28

Twelve years of failed attempts. Twelve years of scheduling appointments with doctors to try to find a way to stop the hemorrhaging. Twelve years of depleted savings, lots of conflicting advice, new techniques, and new medicines—only for her to experience repeated disappointments and financial hardship. Most people would be inclined to give up, embrace defeat, and resign themselves to the fact that they would die in isolation. Why did this no-name woman of Mark's Gospel, only identified by her sickness, get out of bed to make her way to Jesus with no guarantee of healing and the odds stacked against her? It was a huge risk.

We'll imagine the woman's name was Rebecca, and that she was once a beautiful Hebrew woman from a fine family who years before had developed an uncommon, dismaying bleeding. Unfortunately, Rebecca's physical ailment was the least of her problems. The Levitical law of her day—the strict practices that ran the community—labeled her "unclean." The consequence of that label was that she was ostracized and had to live in a primitive shanty outside of town—her bleeding made her unfit for human contact. If she touched another person she would make them unclean. If she touched a chair, a bed, or clothing, she would contaminate the object and the person who touched the object. Gone were invitations to parties, family gatherings, and the local gossip session in the market. She was an invisible person—a ghost living in the shadows. And, of course, as an invisible person she was denied the intimacy of a loving embrace.

For twelve years Rebecca did not feel the soft touch of a hand, nor the caress of human lips. No child would have reached out for her hand or sat on her lap. Her life rhythm revolved around avoiding people. She could only shop in the market in the waning hours of the day, furtively buying what was left or spoiled. Drawing water at the local well was only tolerated when she made certain she would not brush against another person. And since she was deemed unclean, any participation in the religious life of the community naturally was prohibited. Only after the bleeding stopped would she be permitted to go to the tent of meeting with her two doves or two pigeons and be pronounced clean by the priest. Banished by the religious establishment, she was separated from communion with God. And that had been the woman's lot for twelve years.

But on that particularly balmy day, Rebecca had a hunch. Yes, if she could only touch the merest hem of that holy man, Jesus, she would be healed.

Despite all the rejection from her family, neighbors, and religious community, she was still able to act on her incredibly compelling hunch. Despite the verbal and non-verbal attacks that reminded her of her incompleteness and her second-class citizenship, she was able to muster courage. She moved toward a man who could potentially reject her . . . again. Furthermore, touching the clothes of a holy man was risky business. But Rebecca took the risk. She remained true to her hunch. And the Bible makes it clear that we need to notice this woman and learn from her example.

And wasn't it the woman's willingness to overcome in-surmountable barriers that impressed Jesus? Not only did Jesus heal her, but also he went so far as to uphold her as a model of faith—a person from whom everyone could learn. In Jesus' vocabulary the idea of faith was never affirmed in connection to a person's title, position, or theology. The people that Jesus upheld were embodiments of faith, people who acted on hunches that called for courage and a belief in things not seen. With no guarantee of personal healing, our impressive disabled woman acted on what her heart told her to do—touch the garment of Jesus. Because of her willing-ness to reach out, the woman experienced a transforming healing and a moment of growth in faith.

The startling revelation and twist in this encounter is Jesus' final proclamation: "Daughter, your faith has healed you." What's surprising is that Jesus did not attribute the healing to himself. He did not suggest that her healing was his doing. Nor does he suggest that the healing is linked to some magical properties in his clothing. Jesus said that it was the faith of the woman! It was her willingness to act that brought about her transformation, that gave her health, that reunited her with her community and family.

Our ancient and compelling story of Jesus' response presents an interesting paradox of our faith. We just intuitively know that God does not need any help with the miraculous. But in this story we are reminded that there is a human dimension, a human interaction to this question of faith. The woman would not have been healed that day had she not gotten out of bed, gotten dressed, walked across town, and insinuated her way through the crowd to Jesus. She was not passive; she took the initiative. And because of her human initiative, she experienced a miracle.

Isn't this God's great gift of love to humanity? Our choices matter. Our decisions make a difference. Our lives count for something. Our willingness to follow, obey, repress, or ignore hunches can either expand or reduce the presence of God in our lives. Our courage and God's capacity to move in our world can be totally intertwined. God delightfully chooses to work within the restrictions of our humanity by voluntarily working through us. And that's why we are given our holy hunches. We are given our holy hunches because we are the vessels that give witness to God's grace, love, and miracles in his and our world.

When I think of that no-name woman, our Rebecca—the woman who gave witness to courageous faith—I am challenged to consider the obstacles she overcame to start her journey toward Jesus. In order to respond to her holy hunch, she had to confront the social expectations of her day, silence the voices of practicality, refuse to accept her unworthiness, and decide to shut her ears to the naysayers.

Verse 33 in particular gives us a glimpse of this woman's humanity, underscoring her connection with all of us who battle with a sense of inferiority and unworthiness. After she commits this act of obeying her holy hunch by pursuing Jesus, it is evident that doubts begin to seep into her mind. The fact that the Gospel writer records that she was "trembling with fear" indicates that she was far from confident. In the eyes of her community, the bleeding woman had overstepped some pretty enormous cultural and religious barriers, and she knew it. Her mind tortured her, calling up all her fears that reminded her of who she was in the eyes of her culture.

Yet for that brief moment before Jesus said the words "Who touched my clothes?" this woman was able to overcome her sense of inferiority. She overcame the obstacle—that feeling of unworthiness—that hinders so many people from pursuing their holy hunches.

"I'm Not _____ Enough"

I believe that one of the loudest voices squelching our willingness to pursue our holy hunches is that internal one telling us that we are unworthy, inferior, or not good enough to embrace and act upon the promptings of God's spirit. Where does this voice come from? Perhaps parents criticized us for not measuring up to their arbitrary standard? Perhaps teachers berated us for not learning in a particular educational model? Perhaps pastors enjoyed beating us up each week with messages of condemnation and judgment? Perhaps coaches stripped us of our self-confidence for not performing at Olympian levels? Whatever the reason, most of us have experienced the negative poison of those who have held positions of influence in our lives. And they do leave their mark.

The consequence of these encounters can erode our confidence to cross the invisible lines of "authority." We have been taught to show deference to our teachers, our preachers, our physicians, our politicians, and our bosses at the expense of being God's instrument in the spheres of human relations. We look at people of position and compare ourselves as "less than." The bleeding woman had every reason to see herself as unworthy in comparison to Jesus. She had every reason to stay in bed that morning and silence the hunch that was stirring in her soul.

I wonder how often this happens in our own lives. How often do we have a hunch to speak a word of truth to someone older than ourselves, but we silence the voice because of our age. *Who am I? I haven't lived as long as they have.* Or, we may sense that our pastor is doing something wrong, and we need to book a confrontational appointment, but we silence our hunch and think *Who am I? I've never been to seminary. I'm just a biblical novice who doesn't know the Greek or Hebrew.* Or, we may sense that a friend is in some kind of relational situation and needs some advice, but we shy away from the topic because we've had our own relational failings. *Who am I? I've made the same mistakes.* The obstacle of our sense of unworthiness inhibits many of us from obeying the hunches that stir our souls.

I recently preached a sermon on the story of the hemorrhaging woman. I talked about her faith. I talked about her courage to respond to her hunch. About a week later I received a call from a woman in the congregation where I had talked about holy hunches. "I've had a hunch that I am supposed to help you," she began. "I wasn't going to call, because I really don't have anything to offer. But my pastor encouraged me to call." As I talked to this woman, I quickly discovered that she had taught school for numerous years, written curriculum, and trained teachers. She had retired early because of health issues.

By the end of the conversation I was salivating. She oozed with talent and experience—talent and experience that I could never afford to hire. Since I run a school for inner-city children and never have enough resources needed to train our staff, this woman had the potential to truly bless our work and workers. But the whole conversation began with "I really don't have anything to offer." Call it humility. Call it politeness. Call it what you will. The reality of the situation suggests that she was not going to follow her hunch because she did not believe in her abilities and gifts. She was going to derail the whole process of stepping out in faith because she did not believe that her skills had any value for the children in our program. I must ask, "Where does this thinking come from? What are its roots? How many of us abort our hunches because we deem ourselves as having nothing to offer?"

Changing Our Theology, Changing Our Thinking

One of my heroes is Nelson Mandela, the great South African leader who spent much of his adult life in prison because of his opposition to apartheid. Despite difficult and depressing conditions, Mandela never lost his vision for a South Africa that would become a country where whites and blacks live as equal partners. Mandela is an example of someone who never let his circumstances dictate how he felt about himself. Despite being a powerless prisoner, deprived of his freedom and voice, he refused to let the internal voices of despair and negativity triumph. It has been said that Mandela shared the following words in one of his public addresses after he was finally released and then elected as the first black president. Many people have attributed these words directly to Mandela because they capture many of the themes of his life. The actual words, however, were penned by an American writer:

> We ask ourselves, who am I to be brilliant, gorgeous, talented and fabulous? Actually, who are you not to be? You are a child of God. Your playing small doesn't serve the world. There is nothing enlightened about shrinking so that others won't feel insecure around you. We were born to make manifest the glory of God that is within us. It's not just in some of us; it's in everyone. As we are liberated from our own fear, our presence automatically liberates others.[5]

Those are powerful words to embrace. The controversy around whether Mandela actually spoke the words is secondary to the truth of which they speak—a truth consistent with a very significant and central biblical theme. Beginning in Genesis, we are reminded that people are made in the "image of God" (Gen. 1:27)—implying that all people are special, unique, and important to God. In the Psalms we are also reminded that people are made "a little less than God" (Ps. 8:5 RSV) and that people are crowned with "glory and honor." The example that Jesus sets in the Gospels affirms that nobody is a second-class citizen—that all people are worthy of healing and attention no matter how far they have been pushed to the fringes of society. And Paul suggests in the Epistles that in God's reign, distinctions like "Jew," "Greek," "man," "woman," "slave" (Gal. 3:28) are no longer to be used to wield power over another person. This is a rich biblical tradition and says to us all, "You are worthy—not because of your social status, your title, your wealth, your education. You are worthy because you are a child of God."

Once we can truly trust the claim that our worth is found in *who* we are, not in *what* we are, we can begin to freely pursue our holy hunches. We can put aside our feelings of inferiority and cross those social barriers that our culture erects. When we do, pastors can be approached . . . teachers can be challenged with words of truth . . . bishops can be prayed for and blessed . . . bosses can be encouraged . . . broken, alienated, shunned people can approach Jesus. Then our lives will be free to become dynamic agents of God.

➪ 5

Overcoming Pride

Why is it that some people do not bear fruit? It is because they are busy clinging to their egotistical attach-
ments and so afraid of letting go and letting be that they
have no trust either in God or in themselves.

Meister Eckhart

"May I set up a meeting with you?" The voice on the other end
of the phone sounded middle-aged, male, and educated.

"Why is it you want to meet?" I asked, cautiously trying to
show interest. Our receptionist was at lunch, so the caller
had bypassed the usual screening process. Was he selling a
new long-distance service? Life insurance? A better Xerox
machine? I am always a little leery about people who call,
out of the blue, and want to meet.

The man paused. I glanced at my watch, wondering why
I had bothered to pick up the phone. His response was

not exactly what I was expecting. "I want to get a PhD in humility!"

"Pardon me? Can you repeat your request?"

"Yes," my anonymous caller said abruptly. "I'm looking for a PhD in humility. Can you help me?"

Our mission organization offers numerous opportunities for voluntary service, but I was unaware that we were now offering advanced degrees in *humility*. Opportunities to scrub floors? Yes. Service projects? Most definitely. But, a PhD in humility? Not so far. At least the caller got a prize for creativity.

I pressed on and quickly learned that my prospective grad student, Brett Henderson, was a very bright man, one of those intelligent types who excel in the computer sciences and everything else they put their hands to, the kind of guy who learns Greek and Hebrew just for fun. He told me that he had just finished a successful career in the aerospace industry and was about to launch a new business venture on his own. But then something happened. Now Brett wanted to change the course of his life. He wanted to volunteer time to fix things, to roll up his sleeves and do stuff that no one would notice. And he wanted to learn humility.

"Humility?" I asked, hoping to get a little insight into what this was all about.

"Well, I'm certain that this is what God wants me to do," Brett said. "When you get to know me, you'll learn that I'm really arrogant. But now . . . I'd like to learn humility."

Now there's a confession. Not one I hear too often. Most of us have limited skills in the area of introspection, but even there, Brett Henderson had no humility.

Would our organization be the right place for a talented and gifted man to learn humility? Then again, we desperately needed someone to repair things. With hundreds of children using our buildings on a daily basis—imaginatively breaking things, clogging toilets, autographing bathroom stalls—an extra set of capable hands would be a real gift. But there was a problem: if this man was really good and did a great job, our staff and volunteers naturally would love him to death, lavish him with praise and free cups of coffee. Anyone who could unplug toilets, fix broken doorknobs, change the oil in our school buses, now there's someone who could vie for sainthood in our organization. But not anonymity, and certainly not humility.

I began to feel like someone in Vegas ready to take a major gamble. But who could resist a man wanting to earn his PhD in humility? So we made an appointment for him to stop by to inspect our facilities—and for me to discover who this man *really* was.

It turned out that within a week Brett Henderson was hard at work, lugging his toolbox around our campus and looking for things to fix. And yes, as I had guessed, within a month Brett had become the most popular volunteer—"could you fix my door?" "this window?" "this leaky faucet?"—receiving thankful hugs and accolades from everyone.

Certainly, Brett learned important life lessons from volunteering—maybe not those he had initially thought, but he was acting on God's prompting in his life. Brett followed his hunch. And because of his willingness to step out and respond to that holy hunch, a community began enjoying the encouragement of his service. And Brett, little by little, slowly was earning his coveted PhD.

The Obstacle of Pride

I believe that one of the great obstacles to pursuing our holy hunches is personal pride. Like a vice grip, our pride surfaces quickly and squelches our spontaneous responses to God's promptings. How easy it would have been for Brett to excuse God's promptings and say, "Lord, I've got better things to do with my time" or "Come on, these people are only going to see me as a janitor—they're not going to appreciate my intellect, my skills, my wealth." How easy it would have been for his pride to get in the way, thus blocking his important journey, the one he was supposed to travel.

I can imagine myself saying in Brett's situation, "Lord, you want me to do what? Come on, you've got to be joking!" I would think of 101 reasons why *not* to respond to the hunch. "I just finished my doctorate, and you want me to clean toilets? Isn't there a better way to use my gifts? You want me to drive an hour each way to fix doorknobs? Surely there's a better way for me to use my time?"

It's not that I'd be opposed to manual work, to rolling up my sleeves and getting some dirt under my fingernails. But I would sift my hunches through a filter of "good stewardship" and hopefully rationalize the hunch away. Don't get me wrong, I know we should be good stewards of our resources, but it is easy to immobilize our obedience by appealing to religious clichés like "stewardship" or "my God-given gifts" and thus never do anything. In the name of stewardship and practicality, one can easily disguise arrogance and a sense of self-importance. We just deem certain kinds of service work as not God's desire for my life. Rather, we believe that certain work is beneath our status, training, and pedigree. Christians, from the beginning of history, have been confronted by these temptations.

Ponder this: what if the late Mother Teresa of Calcutta had suppressed her hunch to care for the dying in Calcutta by claiming, "These people are going to die anyway; my time and efforts would be better spent on the living." Or if St. Francis of Assisi had said, "You know, my father is one of the most prominent businessmen in Assisi; surely I can use my pedigree for something more important than begging for alms and living like a vagabond." Or if Abraham, the Old Testament patriarch, had responded to the Lord's prompting by claiming, "You know, I'm a successful businessman. I have a good reputation in my community, and it just doesn't make good economic sense to pack up my family and follow a hunch to go to some unknown place." It is easy to rationalize away the promptings of the Spirit using the disguise of "efficiency" and "good stewardship." It's easy to let pride seep into our decision-making process, directing us away from spontaneously following our holy hunches.

C. S. Lewis understood the power of pride when he called it the "complete anti-God state of mind" in his classic book *Mere Christianity*.[6] He insightfully explained that our pride can push us toward believing that we, rather than God, are the center of the universe. Our choices become directed by what *we* feel is best for us—not what God wants for us. How often do we see this pride surface in our lives and the lives of others? God begins to push us in one direction, and our pride begins to push us the opposite way. Consequently, our life's journey becomes anti-God.

For many, pride becomes the ingredient that allows us to forfeit our truest selves—the hunches, the deep longings of our heart, that calling from God—in order to act in a way that maintains or elevates our status in the eyes of our peers and ourselves. As much as we try to deny the truth, we care what other people think of us. Consciously and subconsciously we live in a way that seeks approval from our peers.

When we sense that God wants us to apologize to a colleague at work, our pride counters the hunch, fearing that it might give the appearance of weakness to the others in the office. Our hunch is thwarted by our pride. Or, we choose not to share that word of truth at the church meeting, for it might be unpopular or elicit the scorn of others. Again, our hunch has been thwarted. Or, we may have the opportunity to help a co-worker gain some recognition for an excellent job, but we choose to assert ourselves instead, and we take the credit. Our hunch has been thwarted by a form of pride that is hungry for self-gratification and glorification.

Encouragingly and happily, in the Gospel stories, we find examples of people who overcame their pride and followed their hunches. Their examples give us a chance to see the byproduct of faithfulness in the lives of ordinary people and provide inspiration for our own lives. As a matter of fact, I believe there are unmistakable patterns in the Gospel narratives. The people who sought out Jesus in their belief that healing would come from his hand were those who were willing to cast aside their pride and put at risk their reputations. Those people swallowed their pride and went humbly before the man who had the reputation of rewarding people for their acts of faith. There is no better example of this than Jairus.

A Testimony of Humility

> Then one of the synagogue rulers, named Jairus, came there. Seeing Jesus, he fell at his feet and pleaded earnestly with him, "My little daughter is dying. Please come and put your hands on her so that she will be healed and live." So Jesus went with him. . . . When Jesus was still speaking, some men came from the house of Jairus, the synagogue ruler. "Your daughter is dead," they said. "Why bother the teacher any more?" Ignoring what they said, Jesus told the synagogue ruler, "Don't be afraid; just believe."
>
> Mark 5:22–24, 35–36

The story of Jairus, a synagogue official who begs for the life of his daughter, is a poignant example of humility (Mark 5:21–24, 35–43). He was a man who had authority and power within the religious community of his day. His livelihood was built around the preservation of the synagogue and the maintaining of Old Testament laws. Jairus validating the troublesome Jesus, a renegade healer and prophet who often challenged the teachings of the synagogue, is a vivid picture of humility.

After all, how often in the Gospels does one see a religious leader bow down to Jesus and ask him for a favor? Seldom . . . if ever. Two chapters earlier in Mark, Jesus, on the Sabbath, entered the synagogue and healed the shriveled hand of a man. Needless to say, his act of compassion was not embraced by those in power: "the Pharisees went out and began to plot with the Herodians how they might kill Jesus" (3:6). They made it clear that there was no room for a troublemaker in the synagogue—especially one who did such amazing things. And that event was not an isolated case either. In chapter 7 of Mark, we are told of Jesus going head to head with the religious leadership of his community. This time his disciples were eating with unclean hands (7:2–5). No Jew was supposed to eat unless he had given his hands a ceremonial cleaning. Conflict ensued between Jesus and the religious authorities. No surprise. Don't most of us dig in our heels when our authority and power is challenged—especially if our livelihoods depend on our position of authority?

For example, not many senior pastors surrender their pulpits to an associate who has the gift of dynamic preaching. Imagine, all of a sudden the congregation doesn't want to hear the senior pastor anymore—they just want to hear the young, gifted associate! How long do you think the associate would be around? It would take a self-assured, humble leader to take second place. Or suppose you were a supervisor, and your job was to solve problems for your struggling company. And there was a graduate student in the mail room who had an unbelievably creative mind and probably could change your company around. The problem: if you let this young upstart share her ideas, you'll probably lose your job. How many of us can put our egos aside, seek the help, and potentially jeopardize our future?

Search the Gospels. Is there one story where a religious leader submits, acknowledges, or endorses Jesus as a credible leader? If anything, the religious leaders are threatened by Jesus—threatened that he would become popular among the masses, usurp their control, and open people's eyes to the hypocrisy of the system. They knew that a religious leader bowing down before Jesus would be career suicide. But that's just what Jairus did. He engaged in an act of true humility.

But, because of his daughter's illness, Jairus was desperate. And thus he was willing to do something that none of his colleagues were willing to do; namely, show deference to Jesus and his ability to heal. After all, there were no guarantees that a healing would take place. But Jairus gambled everything on his hunch. Wouldn't it have been easier for him to dismiss his hunch, let his pride stand between his daughter and Jesus, and put the interests of his career and reputation first?

Ponder the radical nature of Jairus's decision. Imagine the reactions from the other religious officials in town when Jairus showed up at the temple. "Hey, Jairus, did we see you get down on your knees in front of that imposter yesterday? Are you joining his crusade?" But Jairus's love for his daughter ran so deep that he was willing to risk everything to save her. He moved on his hunch and discovered that it was his faithfulness that ultimately allowed him to witness the healing of his daughter. It was Jairus's faithfulness to his hunch that allowed him to experience Jesus in a new way. Jairus's life was changed, never to be the same.

People who are willing to "walk humbly with [their] God" (Micah 6:8) and follow their holy hunches are rare. Sure, we Christians quote Bible verses on humility and attend foot-washing services to demonstrate humility. But the people who are willing to listen and act, regardless of the size and importance of the task, are those who experience God in fresh new ways. People such as Jairus risk their careers and reputations. In so doing, they become the people who set the stage for God's unfolding drama in the world.

Sadly, too many times I have sensed God's spirit nudging me to do something out of the ordinary, but I have balked because of pride. I refused to act, because I sensed that obeying would have made me look foolish or vulnerable. Perhaps I needed to apologize to a colleague but was afraid of how it would make me look to the person I had offended. Or I needed to do something for my wife, even though doing it would give the appearance of giving in. Or I felt a nudge toward an act of service that I needed to perform, but I resisted because the job was "too small" or "too dirty" or "not worthy of my qualifications." Pride has the ability to halt us in our tracks, directing us away from what God wants for our lives. Pride hinders our hunches.

The Story of Red

I'm grateful for stories of humble people who remain faithful to their hunches. Gordon Atkinson tells a wonderful story about a parishioner in his father's church.[7] The man's name was Red Davis.

Twenty-five years ago Red Davis was the CEO of a big company in East Texas, one of the major employers in the region.

"Some would say the crowning achievement of Red's life was attaining a high position in such an important company," claims Atkinson. After all, Red was the CEO. He was the man with the power. Red was the one who was invited to power lunches, received the stock options, and had the respect of those who worked under him. In the world's eyes, Red Davis was a success. He had it all, had done it all.

After retirement, however, Red went to his pastor and told him he had a hunch—he felt like he was supposed to serve the Lord. The pastor assumed that Red would be interested in chairing a critical church committee—perhaps finance? Or maybe he would want to steer the capital campaign or become the head deacon. Certainly all that administrative talent of Red's needed to be put to work, all his executive leadership experience needed to be channeled into a place that could have the greatest impact for the growth of the church. Needless to say, the pastor was surprised when Red said no to those opportunities, instead expressing an interest in teaching the three- and four-year-olds in their Sunday school class.

Not surprisingly, Red approached his new task with the same vigor he'd used to run his company. Red would call all the kids in his class every Saturday night, just to ask how their week had gone. He always ended the conversation by saying that he looked forward to seeing them on Sunday morning.

Even so, Red's calls became somewhat problematic for parents, especially those who wanted to sleep in or take the family to the beach on Sunday morning. Now none of the children wanted to miss one of Red's classes.

Kids even began following Red around church, both those in his present class and those from previous years. Church members called them "Red's Army."

For twenty-five years, Red remained faithful to his task. And over those twenty-five years, almost every child in the church was an eager member of one of Red's classes. Everybody knew Red.

Furthermore, if Red ever stood up to speak in a church business meeting, a respectful hush would fall over the congregation. Not just because Red Davis was a successful businessman, but also because he was the gentle Sunday school teacher who was passionate about children's spiritual well-being.

In August 2003, Red died. Gordon Atkinson's father conducted the funeral. As part of the ceremony he asked everyone who had ever been in Red's Sunday school class, or had ever had a child or relative in his class, to stand. Few remained in their seats. Everyone had been impacted by Red.

One of the most telling moments of the funeral service was the testimony of a mother. She told of being in a grocery store with her little boy. They were walking down the aisle between the oranges and bananas when her little boy tugged at her sleeve and said, "Mama, I just saw God!" It was Red Davis. His legacy and memory had been planted deeply in the hearts of everyone who knew him.

The Fruit of Humility

How many retired executives would have followed their hunch to go to the nursery of a church? Not many. But Red did. He probably received disapproving looks and perhaps initially fueled the gossip mill at his church. But Red stayed faithful, and his faithfulness transformed a generation of children.

How many instances of God's presence in the world are blocked because of pride? How many holy hunches are buried in the grave of arrogance? In a world that increasingly exalts false bravado, arrogance, and power it is refreshing to have stories that reflect the impact of humility. And it is those stories that must inspire us to see the bigger picture of what God is doing through humble people.

Listen to God's promptings that may take you down a road less traveled. For hunches can call us to let go of our egos and will break the stronghold of our arrogance. Yes, our hunches may garner strange looks from our friends, gossip from observers, or even condescension from our peers. Yet when we let go of the expectations of others and embrace our full identity as a child of God, we will become like the Red Davises and the Brett Hendersons of the world—men and women who have made a difference in the lives of others. Their humility left space for God to act.

Overcoming the Fear of Foolish Appearances

What matters is whether Christians will dare to risk everything in order to fulfill their function in the world.

Jacques Ellul

Hasn't God made foolish the wisdom of this world?

St. Paul of Tarsus

It was 4:58 on a Thursday afternoon.

How do I know? I remember the exact time because I was supposed to meet my son at his soccer practice at 5:00—a ten-minute drive from my office if I didn't hit any red lights. Time always seems to slip away toward the end of the day.

Now the phone was ringing at the front desk. *Isn't anyone going to pick it up?* I later learned that the receptionist left early that day, not bothering to find a replacement. I picked up the phone . . . and that's not a good idea when you're trying to get out the door.

"Good afternoon." I used my polite, secretarial voice.

"I'm hoping you can help me!"

"I'll try," I replied, glancing at my watch.

"This is going to sound pretty weird," my anonymous caller began. I tensed, sensing this would not be a two-minute call. The big hand on my watch inched past the twelve. I was late. My son would be standing on the soccer field alone.

"About a year ago a group of kids from your youth ministry came to my church. They did some kind of rhythmic dancing. They were really good."

"Oh, that's our Step Team," I interrupted. "Step," as the kids call it, is an urban phenomenon. Instead of using instruments, our young people use their bodies to make sounds and rhythms. Couple that with synchronized movements, and you have a powerful dance expression of creativity. Our team shares their unique skills at many churches each year.

"Yes, that's it, the Step Team," he continued. "Well, there was a young woman who was directing the team when they came to our church, and she was pretty impressive. She had those kids incredibly disciplined. But I can't remember her name . . ."

"It must have been Monique. She heads up our Step Program." Monique is one of those exceptional young people who are extraordinarily gifted with leadership ability. At nineteen, she trained a group of twenty junior high kids with the precision of a military commander . . . without raising her voice. Monique had also overcome tremendous odds—health and family problems. She is one of those special kids who had grown up in our program, benefiting from every program we offer.

"Yes, yes. That's the young woman," he said with excitement in his voice. "Is she still around? Still part of your program?"

"It's interesting that you should call today," I replied. "Monique just called an hour ago. She's graduated from her university and has returned home for the summer. Nobody thought she'd ever make it to college, let alone graduate!"

I did not go on to tell him why Monique had called. She had just gotten home from college to discover that her mother had been evicted from their home because she had not kept up with her monthly payments, and the bank had foreclosed on the loan. Now Monique had no place to live. Feeling a little unsettled, she told me of her desperate need for money to pay a few bills. I've known Monique since she was a child, so she feels comfortable sharing her needs.

"I need some money!" Monique abruptly stated.

"Well, sure, we all do!" I joked, trying to lighten the situation. She chuckled on the other end of the phone.

"I know, I know," she jibed. "I'll pay you back."

In seminary no one ever told me that youth ministry would be about money. And I have over a hundred teenagers knowing my phone number, so it is hard to duck the constant, "Bruce, can I borrow a few bucks?"

"I need a hundred bucks."

A hundred dollars? That stung. I didn't think my wife and kids would enjoy going without groceries this week.

"How about fifty?" I knew we would be bartering, and Monique is a tough bargainer. I started low.

"Seventy-five!"

"Sixty . . . my final offer. But you gotta pay it back," I ended with a gentle reminder.

It was 3:00 when Monique called. Now it was 5:07 and, *coincidentally*, some stranger was on the phone asking if a young woman whose name he didn't remember was still involved in the ministry.

"She's been on my mind for the past year," the caller added, and alarm bells were beginning in my head. "Again, this may sound really foolish . . . but I had this hunch that she might have some financial needs. I want to help her. Do you think she has any critical needs?"

Was I hearing this guy correctly? Was this man, who had briefly met Monique over a year ago (and couldn't even remember her name), calling to see if she had any financial needs? The hair was now standing up on the back of my neck. This was a getting a little weird.

"Does Monique have any needs? Well, um, she just called me an hour ago, desperately needing money for school! And she needs her car repaired so that she can get a job, and she doesn't have a place to live. Plus she wants to apply to graduate school in the fall, and she needs to pay for auto insurance. Yes, she has needs."

Many impoverished young people in our city teeter on the brink of crisis. Unforeseen obstacles appear out of nowhere, derailing dreams and career aspirations. The loss of a job, an eviction notice, or the untimely death of a brother or sister can be enough to tip any scale in the wrong direction. Sometimes a word of encouragement or an unexpected gift makes the difference between collapse and ruin or climbing the next stair. Monique was at that place. She needed a break.

"Well, I'll put a check for a thousand dollars in the mail to you. Feel free to anonymously distribute it to her as you feel it is needed. I hope this will help bring a little stability to her life."

I was dumbfounded and dazzled when I hung up the phone. Not every day does someone call—out of the blue—to help someone whose name they can't even remember.

Before I could really digest the past few moments, I called Monique.

"Do you believe in God, Monique?"

She wasn't sure where my call was going. "Well, to be honest . . . it *is* difficult sometimes," came her serious reply. "Especially when everything seems to be going wrong."

"Wrong? Well, I've got some news that just might bolster your faith. Better sit down," I continued. "A gentleman just called me. He wants to help you financially. So now you've got enough for a down payment on an apartment, with even a little left over for some bills."

"I guess God does care for me," she said with a catch in her throat. "I was pretty anxious about how I was going to make it. This is nothing but an incredible and awesome answer to my prayers."

"One more thing," I added with a hint of glee. "I guess you won't need my sixty dollars."

As I bounded out of my office to my car, I was struck by how the fragile faith of a struggling twenty-two-year-old was strengthened. A holy hunch, when faithfully pursued, made a profound difference. And not only in one life, but in at least three—an aging youth worker who was invited into the middle of a remarkable exchange, a man who courageously acted on God's nudge, and a young woman who has continued to develop into a remarkable person with a heart of compassion and love.

A hunch. It started with a holy hunch.

Oh, and my son got a ride home and was as happy about Monique as I was.

Can I Appear a Fool?

Now, here's one of God's great interventions.

I later discovered that the donor had called from a cell phone during a fifteen-minute coffee break at a medical conference in Atlantic City. He called our office where he knew no one. He just wanted to help a kid whose name escaped his memory. And he wanted to offer a substantial financial gift to someone who may not have even needed it. A therapist or a spouse might deem that kind of behavior as a little . . . well . . . foolish, or at least extravagant.

Think about it for a minute.

What if the person who answered the phone at our ministry headquarters had not left early and laughingly said, "You've got to be kidding. We work with hundreds of kids; how am I supposed to know who you're talking about?" Or, think of the other things that could have happened to Monique. She could have moved to another city, dropped out of school, or lost interest in the ministry. The probability of locating a nameless kid in a sea of hundreds of youth who pass through our programs each day would be akin to hitting the jackpot in Atlantic City twice.

Or, what if the caller had asked a colleague at the convention, "You know, I'm going to make a call to a little youth organization in the inner city and donate a thousand dollars to a young woman whose name I can't remember." Can you imagine the response of the colleague? Strange looks? Laughter on the lunch break? "Have you lost your mind? Why don't you just throw your money to the wind?"

All of those scenarios are probable and could have been very legitimate reasons for not pursuing a hunch. A few minutes of logical reasoning would have repressed the hunch. But fortunately our caller remained true to his hunch and was not afraid to appear a little foolish.

Pursuing a hunch—a holy hunch—might mean suspending one's rational self and taking a chance of appearing foolish. Yet for many of us, appearing foolish is a serious stumbling block and does not sit well with the image we like to project to others. We like to present ourselves as in control, rational, respectable, and level headed. Few of us enjoy being laughed at.

William Sloane Coffin has a wonderful quote: "I love the recklessness of faith. First you leap, and then you grow wings."[8] How many of us are willing to jump first? Call first, and then worry about the response we might get? Give unselfishly, and then worry about the reaction of those who receive our generosity? Most of us, if we are honest, like to make safe decisions—decisions that make us look good rather than foolish.

The Obstacle of Foolishness

And yet, personal foolishness is a part of our Christian heritage.

Throughout the Gospels there is an array of people who follow a hunch and act, well, rather foolish.

The disciples leave their fishing occupation and respond to Jesus' call. Certainly irresponsible and foolish by any measure. Their jobs that have provided their families with food and money were now abandoned for the uncertain promises of a wandering prophet. Foolish? Most would think so.

Jesus risked his reputation by spending lots of time with the outcasts of his community, and in so doing tested the boundaries of the religious professionals. All his love and acceptance of people ultimately invited conflict and rejection and his death. Foolish? Sure.

The woman with the expensive vial of perfume basically dumped her livelihood and most valuable possession down the drain when she poured it on Jesus' head and feet. Foolish? Well, the disciples saw it as an act of waste. Many others thought it absurd.

Then Jesus taught about the last being first, the poor being blessed, the meek inheriting the earth, and blessings for those who are persecuted. Foolish? Well, he didn't stop at that point. Instead he went on to tell people not to worry about things like food, clothing, shelter—but rather to seek the heart of God. Foolish? Mmm-hmm.

The book of Acts recounts the escapades of a community of people who were willing to speak up for their faith even at the cost of persecution, imprisonment, and death. Foolish? You bet.

The apostle Paul picks up the same theme in his letters. To the church in Corinth he reminded the congregation that following Jesus was certainly foolish to those who were wise in the ways of the world.

Without a doubt, there is a pattern in Scripture. When we place the life of Jesus, the teachings of Jesus, the life of the early church, and the words of St. Paul against the backdrop of the world's wisdom and agenda, faith appears to be foolish.

And yet we know that people in the Bible, and saints throughout the history of the Christian church who have responded to their hunches despite the risk of appearing foolish, were powerful expressions of God's presence and witness in the world.

Take St. Francis of Assisi, for example.

St. Francis—God's Fool

Born in the year 1182, St. Francis was raised in a wealthy family and enjoyed all its privileges. His father, a prosperous merchant, expected his son to follow in his footsteps. But after his rather dramatic conversion experience, St. Francis renounced his wealth and took to begging in the streets. To most, including his irate father, he appeared a fool. Yet it was in his willingness to be a fool for Christ that a new strain of Christian faith was birthed. The poor beggar founded one of the most significant movements in the history of the church.

There are a number of stories about St. Francis's willingness to appear a fool. Some of these stories are apocryphal, but even if they do not capture the exact historical details, we know enough about Francis to conclude that they are truthful in the lessons they communicate. One story that captures Francis's willingness to be a fool for Christ takes place in the streets of Assisi. Some children tauntingly approached him and began to shout insults and hurled stones at him. Instead of turning, chasing them away, or threatening to tell their parents, Francis called out that whoever threw one stone at him would be once blessed by God; whoever threw two stones at him would be twice blessed by God; whoever threw three stones at him would be three times blessed by God. At this, Francis was pelted with stones. He then told all the children how much God loved them! Interesting theology.

Most of us would look at that kind of behavior as total foolishness. We would never allow people—especially children—to get the better of us. We would protect our image, guard our reputation, exert our authority. Yet Francis had so completely abandoned his life to Jesus, so allowed himself to be rooted in the identity of Christ, that he had no concern about protecting his reputation or person. Francis left that to God. Francis claimed that the Lord told him to be his poor little fool in this world. Francis believed that although being a fool may appear folly to the world, it is true wisdom in the sight of God.

Our inability to appear foolish is a great obstacle to our acting on our hunches. But why is it so difficult to appear the fool? I believe the answer to this question is centered on the issue of personal identity. From where does our identity as a human being really spring? Do we live our lives trying to preserve a certain image and reputation, always acting within the appropriate social norms of the group from which we are trying to find acceptance? Or is our identity and acceptance rooted in the truth that we are made in the image of God? When this belief is truly embraced, we become free people—people liberated from the perception and expectations of our peers. We become free to act in ways that the world deems foolish. And yet foolishness, for God's sake, is often the gateway through which God's amazing work in the world is done.

PART THREE ←

→ LIVING WITH
OUR HUNCHES

⇨ 7

Igniting Our Hunches

"No eye has seen,
  no ear has heard,
no mind has conceived
    what God has prepared for those who love
him"—but God has revealed it to us by his Spirit.

1 Corinthians 2:9–10

Holy Yellow Pages

"It gave me goose bumps," Bill said, avoiding eye contact with the other board members. "There I was rounding the corner in my Toyota pickup and couldn't believe my eyes—people were lined up for five blocks, parents, grandparents, and children. It was . . . unbelievable!" There was the beginning of a tear in his eye. "We fed 678 families that night. That was one of the best moments of my life. I really felt I was fulfilling God's purpose for my life."

Bill, a middle-aged churchgoer living in an affluent suburb of Philadelphia, had been attending a men's Bible study for years—every Wednesday morning at six! Eight guys and Bill met to study the Scriptures, talk about their lives, and eat donuts and drink coffee. Over the months, key passages in the Old Testament were studied; the Epistles to the churches in Philippi and Corinth were read in their entirety. This little cloister of devoted men explored a good portion of the Bible.

But this year dissecting the Gospel of Luke was creating a problem.

"What are we going to do with this stuff?" Bill asked one morning as he took another sip of his cooling coffee.

Ted Smith, sitting across the circle and nursing his third cup of java, gave Bill a blank stare and replied, "Whatta ya mean, what are we going do about it? Do about what, Bill?" A similar blank stare was shared by the others.

"Well, we've been sitting here for the past hour analyzing this parable of Lazarus at the gate of the rich man," Bill continued with an edge of impatience. "Come on, guys, the message is obvious, isn't it? There's this poor guy and this rich guy. The rich guy walks past the poor guy every day and doesn't do anything about it. Can it get clearer than that?"

Bill paused for a moment. The other guys were caught off guard. The usually calm Bill was getting hot. "I have this sense that we just need to get off our butts and act once in a while. What's the point of coming here week after week and talking about this stuff when it is clear that the message is to get out there and do something? Where are the Lazaruses that *we* walk past each day?"

No one had a comeback; after all, this was a Bible *study*, wasn't it? Studies are about discussion, reflection, and soul feeding. Sprinkle in a few heated discussions about marriage and raising stubborn teenagers, and you have a group that provided a little spiritual infusion once a week. The men had grown accustomed to stoking the old spiritual embers every Wednesday morning but never getting their hands dirty. So Bill's question was perplexing. The study ended with an unusual silence—no talk about the upcoming Eagles game, no jokes, no high fives, just silence.

Bill showed up the following week with a telephone book instead of his Bible. There were perplexed stares from the others. "I went to Washington this past week to observe an organization that feeds poor people," he began. "I asked questions, took notes." The guys looked a little surprised. Bill was really serious. Some were hoping that he had forgotten about his revelation from the previous week and that they could just get back to their discussion. "When I got back, I called an old priest friend of mine, Father Bennigan. He works in an impoverished part of the city. I asked him if there were any families he knew of who needed food. With his Irish humor he replied, 'Is the pope Catholic?' So I went home and made some fliers and distributed them with Father Bennigan in tow, through his neighborhood. The fliers simply and boldly said: 'If you need food, come to church Wednesday night, 7:00 p.m.' And guess what, guys? We're passing out food next Wednesday night!"

Bill chuckled. "And guess what else, guys? We don't have any food to distribute!" he said as he opened to the food store section of his tattered yellow pages and began to tear them out, passing them to the men in the study. "Frank, you call the food stores on this page and see if they'll donate some of their leftover fresh or canned food. Ted, you do the same, here's your page. Jack, you try to get some toiletries."

Within ten minutes all the men had an assignment. Not all were smiling. Some just wanted to get back to their discussion—that was easier. Talking about poor people is far easier than actually helping. Discussing the theological ramifications of Jesus' parables about how people with two coats should share with those who have no coats was much safer than collecting coats for people who were cold. But Bill didn't back down. The men left the study with their assignments.

Within four days, much to the dismay of Bill's wife, his two-car garage was packed with food: pallets of dry goods, cereals, canned goods. "The companies we called were incredibly receptive. There was so much food, I was amazed. The garage was stacked to the roof!" Now the day of reckoning had finally arrived.

"I was a little nervous that night. The guys the next afternoon met me at the house at about four. We loaded our cars with food and the other stuff and headed for the city. As we caravanned our way through the neighborhoods, I was nearly crippled with doubt, with a dread that I had made a huge mistake. What had I been thinking? Where'd I get such a crazy hunch? We rounded the corner at Sixth and State. I couldn't believe the huge crowd that I saw. I was overwhelmed. Father Bennigan told me that people had been there for hours."

That night is still etched in Bill's mind and heart as one of his defining moments. And for the past fifteen years, Bill and a cadre of volunteers have literally fed the hungry, first just one night a week. Then two. Then three. Hundreds of volunteers have been conscripted over the years to distribute the food. Interestingly, Bill just stopped the food distribution a few months ago. "It just isn't needed anymore," he confessed to me. Local pastors and local congregations have picked up the slack and are now helping families get food. Other feeding programs have been initiated.

Sure, Bill's creative and "can do" ministry won't end world hunger; some even criticize his work, saying that such stunts do not alter the structures and systems that create poverty. But at the end of the day, hungry families have been fed (for fifteen years), and momentary suffering has been relieved. I don't know about you, but if I looked into my cupboards and refrigerator and found no food, I'd be pretty happy if someone obeyed their hunch and helped relieve some of the discomfort of hunger.

The Birth of a Hunch

Sometimes our holy hunches come intuitively, other times they need to be sparked. As in Bill's case, the holy Scriptures can become a terrific instrument to create this spark.

I remember a year or so ago when I spoke in the chapel of a very prestigious seminary known for its prestigious academic scholarship, its prestigious degreed professors, and its prestigious student selection. Knowing that there would be Greek and Hebrew scholars in the crowd, analyzing every word I attempted to translate, I was more than a little nervous. After all, what does one say to the literati who are renowned professors of Scripture? My nervous answer was: I'll talk about what I know. So I waded in and spoke about the condition of our churches in the inner city, how they were closing their doors because seminaries had become totally disconnected from the reality of poor neighborhoods. "Blessed are the feet that bring the good news of the gospel," I reminded the audience of Paul's words. "But what happens when those feet don't come to our poor neighborhoods anymore?"

After a solemn benediction, everyone quickly left the magnificent, stately chapel. Amusingly, one elderly professor momentarily paused in front of me and quickly said in a very dignified manner, "I didn't agree, sir, with your translation of the text, but the sermon did have a convicting moment or two." And then he was gone. From his measured world of academia, that was a high compliment! What my distinguished critic revealed was that the Scriptures, no matter how badly we might interpret them, do have the capacity to convict our hearts and minds. By simply listening to the text and meditating on the words, convicting moments can be created. Scripture does have the capacity to ignite certain hunches and compel us to act in certain ways.

My friend Jay puts this idea another way: "Whenever I think I'm about to do something stupid, I pick up my Bible and read the Proverbs." For Jay, the book of Proverbs has the capacity to provide those convicting moments—words that we need to hear so that we can stay on the right track.

That's what happened to Bill. After years of repressing the "convicting moments" created by studying the Scriptures, and after years of dowsing the hunches that were being ignited through Jesus' teachings and parables, Bill finally embraced his hunch and acted. It was the biblical witness that penetrated to the core of his being, reminding him of what it meant to act in a way that truly reflected the heart and nature of God.

Hunches and Loaves

> When Jesus looked up and saw a great crowd coming toward him, he said to Philip, "Where shall we buy bread for these people to eat?" He asked this only to test him, for he already had in mind what he was going to do.
>
> Philip answered him, "Eight months' wages would not buy enough bread for each one to have a bite!"
>
> Another of his disciples, Andrew, Simon Peter's brother, spoke up, "Here is a boy with five small barley loaves and two small fish, but how far will they go among so many?"
>
> John 6:5–8

In order for the Scriptures to ignite the hunches within us, we need to allow ourselves to be influenced by this sacred text in new and creative ways. We need to read the Bible, looking for examples of ordinary people who acted on their hunches, and become inspired by those examples.

Sure, some will criticize this method of reading the Bible, saying, "You're coming to the Scripture with a certain bias." They're partly right. But what we must realize is that we all come to the Scriptures with certain biases. When people read the Scriptures, they may focus on stories that reflect their interests. This is natural. We all come to the Scriptures with our unique histories and needs. We all view the Scriptures through lenses that reflect our biases.

But that's okay, and we need to acknowledge it. But we need also to question our biases. We need to balance our perspectives against the perspectives of others.

Looking at Scripture for examples of people who acted on their hunches can be a helpful exercise and can reveal the important role these examples can play as we attempt to be hunch-inclined people. For instance, the Gospel writer John provided a helpful profile of a young man who was faithful to his hunch.

I often wonder—would there have been a miracle that day if the young boy in John's account of Jesus' feeding five thousand people had covered his sack lunch and hidden it until later in the day? What if the boy, acting on his self-serving adolescent nature, had squirreled away his lunch until sunset? In the dark, nobody would have seen him hungrily devour his fish and barley loaves. I have to confess that I would have been tempted to act in such a way—"What's the point of giving my lunch to Jesus? Sharing my few morsels of food would be pure foolishness—it'd never make a difference with all these people."

Or, I wonder if Jesus' ministry would have changed had the crowds wandered off because of hunger, rather than staying to hear Jesus' teaching. How important was this moment in the ministry and life of Jesus? How important was this moment in the lives of those who stayed to hear his teachings? Obviously the Gospel writer John thinks this moment is pretty important, otherwise he would not have included it in his Gospel.

Of course, we don't know the answer to these conjectures, but what we do know is that one of the great miracles of the New Testament may never have happened had not the forward-thinking teenager (who says teenagers never plan ahead?) packed a lunch. Isn't the boy's willingness to share the significant part of the miracle?

Since all the Gospel writers record the story of Jesus turning a young boy's lunch into a feast for the crowds, we learn that Jesus did not pull miracles out of the air. (John is the only one to attribute the loaves and fish to the boy.) Jesus' miracles are linked to real stuff and real people. According to the witness of Jesus, miracles are the curious result of the divine interacting with the common, whether it is turning common water into extraordinary wine or bringing sight to a blind man. Jesus worked with real matter and allowed people to participate in the process of the miraculous. Take note then: miracles begin and end with the participation of everyday people in everyday circumstances.

Because of this fact, the young unnamed boy in John's account played a critical role in feeding a whole bunch of people, a multitude, a really huge crowd. And Jesus did not produce dinner for five thousand out of thin air. It appears that if the boy had brought forward a bunch of carrots, people would have eaten carrots that afternoon. Had he brought beef jerky in his lunch basket, then, beef jerky it would have been. Possibly a few shrimp and scallops . . . need I go on? Jesus used what was presented.

But the heart of this story is the testimony of a boy willing to act on an impulse—an impulse that urged him to share the crust of bread and the fish he had.

Many of us would dismiss the kind of hunch the boy had as foolish. And many of us would allow our own needs to smother our hunch. But the boy acted on his. And because of his willingness, a small moment in history was altered and preserved to provide inspiration for generations of Jesus' followers. A boy, a few fish, a few loaves made a difference to thousands of people.

Hunches and Feeding the World

Before the gifted and trenchant writer and Christian satirist Mike Yaconelli passed away, he was interviewed by ABC's religion correspondent Peggy Wehmeyer about a program he had initiated called One Life Revolution. His program was his national effort to mobilize American youth to do something significant for children and families in Africa, those dying of starvation and AIDS. His concept was simple: everyone has one life to live—so do something significant and make it count. Now thousands of youth across the country are participating in his program, discovering the impact they can have when their lives and resources are shared with others.

Yaconelli's description of his program's inception is fascinating. He described it this way to Wehmeyer: "We have a hunch and a feeling that if we can get hold of young people, that all of them in this generation are hungry for a revolution. They're hungry for something to do that's meaningful."[9] His national movement that involves young people in acts of feeding and caring for thousands of people around the world started with a hunch. I find it interesting that Yaconelli did not say, "After years of quantitative research, opinion polls, and surveys we decided to start a program that would grip the hearts of young people across the country who want to grow in their faith." No, Yaconelli and some friends had a hunch and decided to act on it.

In the interview Wehmeyer goes on to press Yaconelli on what he thought American youth are looking for today. The man with the hunch responded:

> They're looking for what they've always been looking for—they're looking for meaning, they're looking for somebody to care about them, and they're looking for a calling. To me, we've got generations of kids now who are educated. Many kids get their degree, they go to work one week, and then they're going, "I hate this. I hate doing what I'm doing." That's because nobody ever talks to them about calling. So I think young people today are hungry for a calling, for something that comes along and captures their attention, and captures their whole being.[10]

I am not arguing that Yaconelli conceived the idea for his One Life Revolution in a vacuum. Yaconelli spent a lifetime engaging young people in the things of God. He listened to youth. He understood youth. He studied youth. But he also spent a lifetime studying Scripture, and he realized God's clear and consistent calling for people to help the poor. The undeniable message of God's concern for the poor got under Yaconelli's skin. Then one day he had a hunch.

The Ripple Effect

I did not realize the significance of Yaconelli's One Life Revolution movement—the program conceived on a hunch—until I was talking with a friend.

Steve, a middle-aged financial manager from Pittsburgh, began to share how he was about to travel to Zambia. "Why Zambia?" I asked.

Steve excitedly confided how his son had gotten involved in a program called One Life Revolution. Consequently, the family started supporting a couple of African children through the ministry. They sent money for food, resources, medicine, and educational fees for two orphans in Zambia. Steve was now traveling to meet the children.

Not only was Steve traveling to Zambia, but his son was going to give a year of service in Africa after he graduated from college. One Life Revolution had sparked a vision in his son as well. It had given direction to his life. Steve's son Adam was now bringing his life, his resources, and his time to the One who makes miracles. Just like the boy who had the impulse to share his fish and bread with Jesus, Adam was following his impulse to give to Jesus.

Only God knows the lives that will be touched and fed through Adam.

Only God knows how many other young people and parents will have the opportunity to feed and clothe hungry children.

Miracles happen when people allow the Scriptures to birth hunches in their hearts. The hungry get fed. The sick get healed. And people get to witness the miraculous acts of God's people that transcend the boundaries of reason and rationale.

⇨ 8

FINDING OUR CALLING
THROUGH HUNCHES

The first word he [Jesus] had for all his followers was
not to read, or even pray, but to GO.

George McLeod, *The Coracle*

Often a hunch needs time to germinate.

For instance, Jim Cummings's first inkling of a hunch had
begun the previous year.

He was not just acting on something from yesterday;
rather he was beginning to discover his life's calling. At
fifty-three, Jim was awakening to what God had created
him to do.

But let me fill you in on Jim's background a bit. For the past
twenty years Jim had owned and run a small business—a rug

and floor cleaning business. He had a couple of employees and annual revenues topping out at a couple of hundred thousand dollars. (Not too bad.)

While sitting in church one Sunday morning Jim had a hunch.

He's not sure if it came during the waning moments of the sermon, during the third verse of "Great Is Thy Faithfulness," or while daydreaming during the pastoral prayer. But the hunch was like this: could he use his love of the wilderness to enrich the lives of inner-city kids? Jim spent any free weekend he could out in a canoe or hiking in the woods. The idea had been nagging at him for years, but that particular Sunday the hunch was really strong. It came to him: *Why not share something I love with kids who might not have the opportunity to have such an adventurous, awesome experience? I'll bet there are hundreds of kids interested in joining an outdoor club!*

And that's where our organization for kids came in. Over the course of the year Jim encouraged more than a dozen UrbanPromise teens to visit the Cranberry Bogs camp at the edge of the Chesapeake Bay and canoe in the New Jersey Pine Barrens. The youth loved it.

"Now I'm ready to quit my job," Jim said excitedly as he laid out his plan on my desk—a professionally bound ten-page proposal. "I know it sounds a little crazy, but I'm going to take this outdoor club to a whole new level, do more excursions with a historical, environmental bent to them. We'll read travel and adventure books, then visit the places of significance we read about. I'm gonna call it Expeditionary Learning. How'd you like that?"

Expeditionary Learning? Wow!

There was excitement in Jim's voice; he seemed to have a new lease on life, a kind of rebirth—a midlife epiphany. He was ready for a new venture. "I'm passionate about this," he nearly shouted. "I'm going to get an old school bus, take out seats in the back, and install a small kitchen. There'll be a mobile classroom, and the world will be our science lab. We'll teach life skills, making the young people's education hands on."

Had Jim just walked in off the streets and shared his dream with me, I would have rolled my eyes and gently guided him out. I'd already talked to too many people in my office who had a starry-eyed answer to the world of poverty and America's inner-city communities. But Jim was different. I had watched him work with our kids for over a year—he showed up on time, his monthly excursions were well planned and thoughtful, the students liked him, and he had their trust.

Jim and I had casually talked about his hunch to explore the beauty of nature with city kids. But now he was talking about a converted bus, a hundred-thousand-dollar budget, and cross-country trips. Indeed, he was talking about a major career shift.

During the next year, Jim had his inborn gifts and intuitions affirmed. His initial hunch to share his love of the great outdoors and the awesomeness of God's creation had been initiated. He had seen the kids' eyes light up when they discovered the Big Dipper and the infinite galaxies of stars in ebony skies. He heard the sheer joy of laughter when boys saw the wild horses on Assateague Island; he treasured the conversations with kids paddling canoes on the Delaware. Jim's gifts had been affirmed. And it was because of his willingness to act on his hunch that Jim was now discovering his life's calling.

Finding Our Calling

> When Simon Peter saw this, he fell at Jesus' knees and said, "Go away from me, Lord; I am a sinful man!" For he and all his companions were astonished at the catch of fish they had taken, and so were James and John, the sons of Zebedee, Simon's partners.
>
> Then Jesus said to Simon, "Don't be afraid; from now on you will catch men."
>
> Luke 5:8–10

So, how do we find our life's calling?

Is it possible to spend our time during our short life on earth to use our talents, passions, and gifts for God's purposes? Do revelations come to us like a bolt of lightning—in an audible voice in the night?

Sometimes.

In my experience, however, a life calling is seldom discovered in an arrow-to-target way—not even for those who earnestly seek to align their lives with the intentions of God. Most of us, rather, tend to stumble into those places where a deep connection between our truest selves and our work takes place.

But moving toward discovering this place of deep connection has a beginning.

Pursuing a hunch plays a significant role in the finding of our purpose.

Did not the journey of the Old Testament's Abraham begin with a hunch? The old patriarch stumbled along from one crisis to another to discover his calling as the Father of God's people! Likewise, Moses painfully grew into his role as leader and deliverer of his people. Didn't the prophet Jeremiah begrudgingly accept his calling as the one who must speak strong words to his people?

Then there's the New Testament. The apostle Peter. We first meet Peter when he's on a boat, eking out a living as a fisherman. According to Matthew's recollection, the fishing that morning had not been particularly good; in fact, it had produced nothing. (Those of us who have spent hours staring at the end of a dormant fishing pole know the feeling—fishing, when nothing is biting, is boring, if not infuriating.)

But then someone new in the area—and certainly not a professional fish monger—came along and offered a suggestion. "Put out into deep water and let down the nets for a catch" (Luke 5:4). Most expert fishermen that I know would have just laughed at the suggestion—especially from a novice, land-loving religious teacher. What does he know about tides, currents, and feeding patterns of fish? The alpha-male ego would take over, nod politely, and chuckle under his breath, "What does a man who never spent a day in his life on a boat know about catching fish?" (From what we subsequently learn about Peter, this kind of response is not beyond the scope of his personality—he was the guy who aggressively cut off a man's ear when his sense of security was threatened. The Gospel writers portray Peter as an aggressive, impulsive, strongly opinionated, sometimes ornery type.)

Yet there is a genuine reverberation deep within Peter when Jesus instructs him to change his fishing strategy. Perhaps Peter's willing compliance grew out of desperation, perhaps discouragement. Was it something he heard in Jesus' teaching to the crowds on the beach? No. Something deeper. Peter had the intuitive sense that his fishing prowess, his whole career might change if he followed this suggestion. He responded to Jesus' gently authoritative command, and to his surprise the nets became full—more than full.

But for me, the next part of the story is even more fascinating.

After the fishing miracle, the value of Peter's business increased by 57 percent. His monthly revenue shot up to unexpected highs; investors took note. Men in the other fishing boats considered joining the Simon Fish Emporium crew. Not only would his family eat well that month (no more macaroni and cheese, thank goodness), but there would be money left over—enough for a Mount Zion getaway, a bonus for the help, toys for the nieces and nephews, and a Home Depot set of tools for himself. Peter's business had the jump-start it needed. Or as a venture capitalist might say, the business was infused with the necessary cash to take it to the next level.

But stop a moment! Listen.

The itinerate preacher cum fishing strategist calls out, "Don't be afraid, Peter. From now on you'll catch people."

And here's the question: why does Peter walk away from a business that has just seen record revenues? With a newly cash-infused bank account, why would Peter throw it all away on a guy who was offering no salary package, no benefits, and no retirement plan? Why would he walk away from a burgeoning business that would bring him security, a sense of identity, and honor within his community?

Could it be because deep within Peter's soul there was an existential discontent?

Sure, Peter could fish for the remainder of his life and do well; for the next forty years he could wake up every morning and go fishin'. Oh, there'd be good days. And bad. (There are impetuous, ferocious storms on the Sea of Galilee.) But as a successful fisherman, Peter could very handsomely provide for his family, be thought well of on the board of the Sabbath school, watch his kids grow and become the leaders of the local synagogue. Hey, don't rock the boat!

Like many people who desire to spend their life's energy in activities more meaningful and significant than simply surviving, Peter found that Jesus' prompting to come and "catch people" resonated deeply within his soul.

When Jesus unequivocally asked him to leave everything and follow, Peter was true to his hunch. (I use the term *hunch* here rather than *calling* because Peter had absolutely no clue about the journey he was about to embrace.) His hunch was a deep sense that journeying with this earthy, unique holy man would lead to a place where life had more purpose, where life would be a fulfilling adventure.

Yet, what did Jesus really offer Peter? Nothing definitive! Just a vague promise that Peter would now catch people—whatever that meant. Peter would now have to move forward by faith with an intuitive sense that this new life direction would provide something he could never have discovered on his fishing boat.

Interestingly, the practical details of life were never discussed between Jesus and Peter. There was no discussion that we know of about travel plans—"where shall we go first?" No discussion of life's basic necessities—"who'll pro-

⇧

vide meals?" No discussion about career potential—"what's my job description . . . and, oh, how do I fit into the organizational chart?"

Impulsive Peter acted solely on his hunch that this man Jesus, and his promise, could be trusted. Peter could release his old life; he could abandon everything that gave him a sense of security and identity.

Yet it was Peter's response to this hunch that called him to first trust the call that Jesus had made. It was Peter's obedience to this hunch that put him on a new, less traveled road, on a new journey that would radically change his life. It would be a journey of success and failure. It would be a journey of joy and sadness, a journey of deep pain (he could not have known then that he would be killed), and a journey of deep spiritual discovery. And, most importantly, it would be a journey on which he learned of his frightening inadequacies and God's incredible, loving power.

But it began with a hunch.

Peter's Moment of Radiance

> When they saw the courage of Peter and John and realized that they were unschooled, ordinary men, they were astonished and they took note that these men had been with Jesus.
>
> Acts 4:13

Was there a moment in Peter's life when it all came together? Was there a moment when we can say that Peter's unique gifts, unique personality, and unique history all converged around a God-inspired purpose? Was there a season of his life that you and I can point to and say that Peter really fulfilled God's purpose?

Perhaps it was the moment Peter cut off the ear of the high priest's servant to protect the newly arrested Jesus from tyranny? Yes, that was Peter's moment of glory and ultimate purpose—a chance to save his Master! Oh, but wait. Jesus' response dictates otherwise. And sadly, Peter still did not fully understand the mission.

Or was it the moment Peter denied Jesus three times? Wasn't that merely a brilliant acting job of self-preservation, a chance to outlive Jesus and ensure that his wise sayings, teachings, and legacy would be preserved? I don't think so. Jesus did not need Peter to carry on his name.

Surely Peter's finest hour was when he healed the crippled man outside the temple and claimed with confidence, "I do not have silver or gold, but what I do have I give you." With that, the man was instantly healed and gleefully danced away, praising God. The former fisherman now had become someone who could do more than transform a fish into a filet. Peter now had the capacity to be a significant, incredible agent of change. Well, we'll see.

I think the defining moment of Peter's life was when he defended his faith with boldness and integrity to the Sanhedrin—those educated, intimidating rulers and elders. At that point in his life, Peter was a long way from unreliable, meager catches, leaky boats, and the gruff curses of his fishing buddies. He was now living beyond his human capabilities. Witnesses confirmed the obvious as Luke wrote in Acts: "When they saw the courage of Peter and John and realized that they were unschooled, ordinary men, they were astonished and they took note that these men had been with Jesus" (4:13).

What an evolution in Peter's growth! Fortunately, the Gospel records of Peter's life are transparent and reveal both his failures and successes. But the later records of Peter's life do reveal a man who had changed. They reveal a man who had discovered the fullness of his God-created humanity. Yet in order for him to arrive at this destination—this place of human and divine convergence—he acted on a hunch. He had acted on a promise from a man he did not know, went on a journey that had no clear destination, and put his trust in a hunch that nudged him toward Jesus.

Taking the First Step

Too many people never fully discover their God-given gifts because they basically spend their lives saying no to their hunches; they never take the first step that leads to the second then the fortieth and the hundredth. They never begin the journey that leads to the discovery of how they are intended to live.

Peter would never have discovered that he had the gift of preaching, the gift of healing, the gift of sharing his faith, had he not said yes to his first hunch. My friend Jim never would have discovered that his love for the outdoors would become a transformative instrument for city kids had he not moved out of a church pew one Sunday, made a phone call, and driven into our neighborhood.

I have no idea where Jim will be five years from now. But, I do suspect he will be more fully engaged in his expeditionary learning adventures—perhaps trips to the Amazon, the Rocky Mountains, or the Grand Canyon. I suspect, despite this aging season of his life, he will be more alive and vigorous than he has ever been, with a pantheon of teenagers calling out his name as they give their valedictorian speeches.

⇨ 9

DISCERNING OUR HUNCHES

> It became important for the church of Christ to find
> a way clearly to distinguish between true and coun-
> terfeit spirits.
>
> Jonathan Edwards

The phone kept ringing. I reluctantly struggled awake and
saw through slit eyes that it was one in the morning. I groped
for the receiver. "Hello," I said groggily.

"Bruce? Sorry to disturb you. It's Brian." My heart skipped
a beat, and my stomach tightened. These are never good
calls. "One of our interns is in the emergency room. You
need to come."

"What happened? Who?"

"The doctors don't know exactly what's wrong. It was
Jenny." Brian, our program director, stumbled on. "But

they think she'll probably be okay. She had some kind of seizure."

Within what seemed like minutes I bolted through the glass doors of the emergency unit. The orderly intercepted me and assured me that everything was okay—just a little scare. But Jenny had gone into some kind of coma. Low sugar? An allergic reaction? The doctors were checking her medical history. They felt sure that she would be released in the morning.

I visited briefly with Jenny, said a quiet prayer for her, and encouraged her to get some sleep. Thirty minutes later I was back in the lobby drinking coffee with Brian. I glanced at the clock: two-thirty.

"Bruce, we've got a problem," Brian began as I stirred sugar into my cup.

"Yes, I know. But the doctor assured me everything for Jenny was going to turn out okay." I sighed, trying to reassure us both. "Let's just be thankful that it wasn't more serious."

"No, Bruce, I don't mean about Jenny." He paused as I took a gulp of my still too-hot coffee. "I mean . . . it's about what happened back at the house tonight."

"The house? What happened at the house?" Now I was alarmed. A young woman, in a coma, rushed to the hospital wasn't enough for one night?

"Jenny started complaining around eleven last night that she wasn't feeling well. Everyone was concerned even though she kept reassuring us that everything was okay. Then Jenny collapsed on the couch. Her eyes began to dilate. Our house director yelled to call 911."

"Well, I'm glad *someone* knew what to do," I interrupted, holding my exasperation in check.

"Then one of the other students, Eric, shouted in a very agitated manner that we *shouldn't* phone 911." Brian paused.

Eric? Wasn't he one of our new summer interns, about nineteen years old? I tried to picture him. Hadn't he just arrived two days ago? I hadn't had the opportunity to meet him yet, but his application and references had checked out just fine, hadn't they? But now? "He didn't want to call 911? Why?"

"Because he . . ." Brian stumbled momentarily. "He *sensed* that this was not a medical issue, it was a spiritual one. Eric said—with intimidating intensity—that he could feel a demonic presence in the room and that we all just needed to pray over her."

I choked on my coffee. For years I have been recruiting young men and women to serve as urban missionaries. I have placed them in teams in houses or apartments in our urban neighborhoods and taught them how to do outreach in the community. We carefully screen our interns, but there are risks. Our interns come from an assortment of theological and denominational backgrounds, which makes the dynamics of the households interesting—to say the very least. But in all my years I had never had a situation where someone's life was in jeopardy because of another person's religious interpretation of an event.

Brian continued to recount the story. "'Can't you see,' Eric was nearly yelling now, 'this is the work of Satan—Jenny's in bondage. She doesn't need a doctor, we just need to pray!' I told Eric firmly that he could pray for Jen all he wanted, but that he would do it in the next room. But he wouldn't go, so I ended up physically pushing him out of the room while the others called 911. Needless to say, the other students were really unnerved."

At this point I could not have been prouder of Brian. He did what needed to be done. Confronting a peer—especially a peer bubbling with inappropriate religious zeal—can be a difficult challenge for a group of twenty-year-olds.

"Well, then it really got interesting," Brian continued. I wasn't sure I wanted to hear about *interesting*. "After the ambulance came and took Jen to the hospital, Eric went out on the front stoop and began to roar like a lion!"

"Roar like a lion? A lion?" I was incredulous. It's one thing to forgo medical treatment in the name of prayer—it is another to be roaring like a lion in the heart of the inner city at midnight. This was turning into a community relations nightmare. Not only was the staff unnerved by their peer's behavior, but now the whole neighborhood was thinking that the Christian missionaries at the end of the block were nuts!

"Brian, bring Eric to my office this morning at nine. I'll see what's going on here." I laid my hand on his shoulder and assured him of his wise handling of a difficult and perplexing situation. "Now let's go home and try to get a few hours' sleep, if we can."

Discerning Our Hunches

At nine the next morning, Eric, a confident, almost swaggering young man, knocked at my office door. I greeted him and offered him a seat. "Tell me about last night—event by event." Eric quite comfortably told me that Jen's problem was more spiritual than physical.

"And the roaring?"

Eric went on to tell me about his encounter with the Lion of Judah on the front stoop at 424 West Fourth.

"It was the most intense spiritual moment of my life," Eric said with total sincerity. "I never felt so close to the Lord. It was beautiful, personal. No one can discredit it; it was so real."

"I'm not going to discredit your moment," I said softly. "But we need to look at your behavior in the broader context."

I do not come from a charismatic tradition, but I do believe in the movement of God's Spirit in the world: I also believe with the apostle Paul that the gifts of the Spirit have a central purpose—they unite and strengthen communities of faith. Spiritual gifts and unusual spiritual expression always serve a larger purpose. Whether Eric had a valid spiritual experience was not the central issue here. The larger issue on the table was how his experience impacted his community—a community of believers that had a specific calling to serve and love children in an impoverished neighborhood, in the name of Jesus. Eric could have been acting on a hunch. But did his hunch enhance God's broader ministry to children and teens in his neighborhood?

"Eric," I began slowly and seriously, "I am not here to question your beliefs. But I need to be very frank. Each summer I hire leaders to live in our staff houses. After an extensive series of interviews and prayer, I place the young men and women in leadership positions because of their wisdom and good judgment. In the case of life and death situations, I need to be assured that counselors, like you, will follow the leader's directions. Your leader discerned that Jen's situation needed medical attention. You needed to back that decision.

"I also believe, Eric, that God gives us faith-enriching experiences to build up our communities. But your behavior last night has put fear into all of your colleagues—they are now nervous about living in the same house as you. They are concerned about entrusting children to your care. They're afraid that if there's a situation where a child's life is in danger, you might not act in a way that serves that child's health and welfare."

Eric stared at me in silence.

"And further, Eric, we've worked in this community for eight years. We've tried to build trust with the neighbors so they will send their children to our programs. I just find it hard to believe that God would have you do something that might undermine all those years of trust. Roaring like a lion might have been an important experience for you personally, but I think it could ultimately damage the reputation of our ministry in the community."

I continued. "Spiritual gifts are given to us so we can strengthen the body and witness of Christ in the world, not undermine them. Sometimes our personal experiences need to be tempered by the larger vision of what God wants to do."

Eric could not accept my point of view. He abruptly said thank you and that he would be leaving. It is my hope that by now he has matured and grown in his faith.

But, my encounter with Eric did raise a number of questions about hunches. When are they valid? Do they ever conflict with the greater good of what God is trying to do? How do we discern these intuitive inklings as to whether they are really from God or something that is fabricated in our own psyche to meet our own emotional needs?

Checking Our Hunches

Those who read the annals of church history know that there have been, unfortunately and sadly, very bad things done in the name of God. Sincere, pious, churchgoing people have acted on hunches that have brought scores of people destruction and ill will. Hunches have burned innocent people at the stake, sparked crusades, and led to genocide—all justified by someone's interpretation of God's calling. Misguided hunches have also caused people to lose their life savings, to make harmful career choices, to split churches, and to ruin relationships. Acting on misguided hunches can do a lot of damage to us, our families, our friends, and our communities. Is there any doubt as to why John would write to his community:

> Dear friends, do not believe every spirit, but test the spirits to see whether they are from God, because many false prophets have gone out into the world.
>
> 1 John 4:1

Misguided hunches can also diminish the work and witness of God in the world. So the question becomes: is there a way to discern our hunches, or the hunches of others, so as to ensure that they are in line with the intentions of God?

In order to find an answer to this critical question, we must look for patterns and themes in the Gospel narratives—patterns and themes that might act as a lens that filters our own hunches, ensuring that they are "holy" rather than, let's say, unholy or distorted or just a little off kilter.

Here are a few ideas, learned from Jesus' encounter with people acting on their hunches, that will help assist our discerning process.

Number One: Hunches are not given for the sake of meeting my own ego needs.

Lest I sound too abstract, let me share from Mark 10:35 an example of a misguided hunch—Jesus' encounter with James and John. In those few verses we meet two brothers who have what we'll call a hunch. They consequently asked Jesus if they could occupy two very special seats in God's coming, eternal glory. (Modesty was not their forte.) In verse 38, Jesus basically asked them to reconsider their request because they didn't really know what they were asking. Jesus then reminded them and the rest of the disciples about the intriguing reversals in his teachings: greatness does not come with priority seating; greatness comes by serving. The motivation behind the request (or the hunch) of James and John was obvious. They wanted to separate themselves from the other disciples. They wanted a place of special recognition. They wanted to fulfill their own ego needs. Jesus used that encounter to remind his disciples of his teaching.

The exchanges between Jesus, James, and John are helpful for us in discerning our own hunches. Hunches that call us toward the exaltation of self are not holy hunches. Hunches that call us toward places of elevated status do not capture the essence of Jesus and his priorities for his followers. Thus, James and John were reminded that greatness comes from serving and not from privileged seats of honor. Any hunch that is motivated by a need to receive special recognition always needs to be questioned.

James and John's principle of "me first," if expanded, certainly would include the idea that our hunches should be questioned if the goal is simply the accumulation of personal wealth, better cars, bigger houses, signs of superior spirituality and success—symbols that provide an exalted sense of our worth. I am particularly afraid of those who say, "God's given me a hunch to invest my life's savings in XYZ Company, promising tremendous financial return." Against the backdrop of the Gospel narratives, I find no story, event, or teaching that would support this thinking. If the Scriptures are a lens through which we can evaluate the legitimacy of our subjective experiences, then we evaluate our hunches against the story and teachings of Jesus. If our hunches are motivated by the craven promise of rewards, we had better reevaluate their source of inspiration.

And those "rewards" are not only limited to those desiring financial reward and professional advancement. It is easy for our ego and personal ambition to skew our motivations in any vocation—especially in religious work. I remember reading a quote from the late Mother Teresa of Calcutta after she had received her Nobel Peace Prize. In a letter to former senator Mark Hatfield, if I remember correctly, she wrote, "Please pray for me. Pray that I will not let go of the hand of Jesus while I serve behind the disguise of ministering to the poorest of the poor." Mother Teresa was acutely aware of how distorted our sacrificial service, our callings, and our hunches can become—even when our intentions are noble. Mother Teresa knew the dangers of our ego and how our motivations for serving God could easily separate us from an authentic walk with Jesus.

Questioning our motivations is tricky and complex, as we are often blinded to our own ambition. But if we become people who saturate ourselves in the stories of Jesus and begin to truly understand the essence of his message—loving others, traveling the second mile, turning the other cheek, serving sacrificially, being content with second place—perhaps then, and only then, will we develop the capacity to check our hunches.

Hunch Check: Who will ultimately benefit from this hunch? Is this hunch just about making me look better in the eyes of my friends and peers? Am I using the disguise and language of spirituality to fulfill my own insecurities? Does the desired outcome of this hunch align itself with the central message of Jesus' life and teachings?

Number Two: Holy hunches are given for the benefit of other people—especially to help those alienated from the broader community.

One of the startling consistencies unveiled in the Gospels is that a holy hunch often moves a person toward Jesus on behalf of another person. Although there are exceptions to the pattern, there are numerous examples of selfless people acting on behalf of others. Those characters who find themselves moving into the presence and space of Jesus are doing so to help another human being: four guys for their paralyzed friend, a desperate father for his dying daughter, a distraught mother for her demon-tormented daughter, a loyal centurion for his suffering servant, or a concerned son-in-law for his feverish mother-in-law.

Advocacy on behalf of others should be one of the filters that test our hunches. For a hunch to be truly holy, its intent should be to help those who have been relegated to the far corners of society or alienated from the church. When I think of Daryl and Darrel providing chemistry lessons for inner-city teens, Jim Cummings sharing his love of the outdoors with high school students, Bill feeding hungry people, or an anonymous donor trying to help a deserving kid get on her feet, I see Christians who are responding in a way that blesses and enriches the lives of those who have little. When God comes alongside of those who pursue a hunch on behalf of another, incredible things can happen. It seems to me that the Gospel writers wanted to affirm this message to their readers: Jesus converts hunches—embraced and pursued on behalf of those unable to advocate for themselves—into opportunities for the miraculous to be released in the form of healing and the restoration of abandoned people to relationship with God and others.

Hunch Check: If you write down your last ten hunches in your journal, would you see a pattern? Would the pattern suggest that your hunches are for the benefit of other people? What kind of people?

Number Three: Holy hunches are not always an end in themselves. They are part of a journey that should deepen our relationship and understanding of what it means to follow Jesus.

Think of the disciples. They acted on a hunch when they left their nets and turned their backs on their livelihood. They had absolutely no idea about what they were committing to. Their hunch to follow Jesus turned out to be a call to grow, learn, and give witness to the presence of God in the world. Their hunch to follow Jesus ultimately led to hardship and eventual death.

If we think a holy hunch will lead us toward easier lives without pain and without hardship, we will be disappointed. Authentic hunches, rather, will stretch our faith, lead us to places where dependence on God is critical, and challenge us to deepen our commitment to living like Jesus in our world.

The late Oscar Romero reminds us that pursuing hunches is not just about personal blessing. Romero reminds us of the potential growth that comes from pursuing our hunches on behalf of those less fortunate. Selected by the church hierarchy to be the Archbishop of El Salvador because of his bookish, quiet demeanor, Romero became an outspoken critic of his government because of their treatment of the poor. Pursuing his hunches for truth and justice ultimately cost him his life. In Romero's case, the resultant miracle of faithfulness to the Spirit's hunches was the transformation of his character. The year before his assassination he preached:

> It makes me sad to think that some people don't evolve ... Christianity is not like that, and neither is the gospel. It has to be the leaven of the present time.[11]

In another sermon he added:

> Those who, in the biblical phrase, would save their lives—that is, those who want to get along, who don't want commitments, who don't want to get into problems, who want to stay outside of a situation that demands involvement of all of us—they will lose their lives. What a terrible thing to have lived quite com-

fortably, with no suffering, not getting involved in problems, quite tranquil, quite settled, with good connections politically, economically, socially—lacking nothing, having everything. To what good? They will lose their lives.[12]

Holy hunches call us to involvement with our world—to speak truth, to take risks, to advocate justice, to love lavishly, and to love the unpopular. Engaging this kind of journey will lead to extraordinary personal growth. And yet it is in the midst of this gospel living that we begin to discover our calling and purpose for our historical period.

Hunch Check: If our hunches lead to conflict and discomfort, will we remain faithful to them? Have past hunches led to growth in character and faith? If so, what were those hunches? How might I embrace similar hunches in the future?

Is My Hunch of God?

Responding to holy hunches is a subjective enterprise. There is no exact or detailed formula, pattern, methodology, or program that can ensure that our hunches are truly holy. That fact is both exciting and terrifying. Exciting because we have been given this wonderful opportunity and freedom to listen to God's Spirit and respond to its holy promptings with faithfulness. It is terrifying because we are human beings who are subject to selfishness, petty insecurities, and fear, and are fully capable of missing God's intention for our lives. Therefore, we have the capacity to be agents of healing and restoration—or the capacity to be agents of hurt and destruction.

Reflecting on the stories of Jesus' response to those who acted on their holy hunches can increase our possibilities of becoming agents of healing and restoration. When we respond to hunches that promote God's interests in the world, and not our own, we will reduce the possibility of our abusing a wonderful, exciting, and blessed gift.

⇨ 10

What to Do with a Hunch Gone Wrong?

It is commonly thought that if we begin a project for the Lord, the pieces will fall into place. It doesn't work out that way. . . . Disasters befall projects of the good spirit, as well as those of the bad. Success has never been a sign of God's will . . . it seems to me a sure sign that a certain project is the work of God is if we have the grace to struggle on without bitterness in the face of difficulties and frustrations.

Benedict Groeschel

December was meanly cold that year. A recent nor'easter blizzard had brought the mercury down to abnormally cold conditions for the New Jersey and Philadelphia's Delaware Valley. Few ventured from their homes, and certainly not for a Sunday evening church service. Consequently, attendance that night was minimal at our little Baptist church.

But there we were—Helen, Cleve, John, and I—the last stragglers chatting in the vestibule, about to lock up the church on the Sunday before Christmas, each reluctant to move out to brave the piercing wind and get into our cold cars.

Curiously, I had preached a sermon on the Good Samaritan. At Christmas? Obviously, I had disregarded the liturgical calendar and had fearlessly ventured into a familiar story—one that we all had heard from early Sunday school years. But I was pretty pleased with it, nonetheless.

There was a knock on the sanctuary door—or more of a desperate pounding. We were startled, and none of us moved. What kind of person would be outside on a night like this?

I pushed the safety bar, and in blew a bearded, middle-aged man and his tattered, bluish, windblown wife. The man's tobacco-yellowed teeth, greasy brown hair, and frantic eyes revealed a desperate man in desperate times. "Can you help me and my wife?" he blurted, eyes watering from the cold. "We've been sleeping in our car, and we'll freeze to death if we stay out tonight." He moved right to his point. "Thirty bucks, and we could get a motel room down the street!"

Little did our shivering, disheveled guests know that we had just been primed for their visit, the benevolent Samaritan's story still reverberating in our memories. No chance any of us could turn our backs . . . especially the preacher. Everyone looked to me.

"Well, um, what about sleeping here in the church?" (My wallet was literally empty.) "It'll stay warm until morning."

Unlike the Samaritan, I didn't have a single dime to give the innkeeper.

"Our insurance policy doesn't cover people sleeping in the facility," Mr. Smith, one of our older deacons, said with a frown. I decided to hold back on a confrontational theological discussion on the purpose of the Church—something like "These are not really our buildings, and Jesus might be happy if we really turned our sanctuaries into, well, sanctuaries, places of rest and refreshment for the weary and broken."

My friend Helen slipped an envelope into my hand and whispered, "This should cover them for the night."

I motioned the homeless man aside and passed him the thirty dollars.

"Why don't you come back in the morning around eight?" I added. "We've got some cleaning that needs doing. I'll pay you for that."

Surprisingly, the man and his wife showed up the next morning ready to work, rested and clean. They looked like new people. I showed them the kitchen. They made a pot of coffee and fried some eggs. With food in their stomachs, they were ready to work. I must confess that I didn't get my hopes too high, because it had not taken me long in my pastoral career to realize that needy people who knock on church doors for loans with a promise to return the next day with full payment seldom translated into reality.

But by nine in the morning Tom and his wife were at the door. They swept, vacuumed, cleaned bathrooms, and dusted. Even being a skeptic I was impressed. Things were looking good. I gave the couple fifty dollars and a box of food and invited them to return the next day. The next day the couple showed up, worked hard, and seemed to appreciate the opportunity. It was a win-win deal. "We want to put some money down on an apartment," Tom said after the third day. He began to open up a little. He shared his history and some of the hardships of his life—foster homes by the age of eight, dropping out of school by fifteen, a string of unlucky breaks. Life had been far from easy. "I just need a break," he inferred during one of our exchanges. "Someone who'll look past my mistakes." I liked that.

By day three we advanced to some bigger jobs—stripping and waxing floors and varnishing the church pews the neighborhood kids had scratched up. Tom had some real know-how, and I was getting much-needed maintenance completed. Even my most disgruntled trustee might smile when he sat in his favorite, now dusted and polished, pew the following week.

Then I had a hunch.

"Our missionary house is empty for another two weeks," I encouragingly said during one of our chats. "Our workers have gone home for their three-week winter break. Why not use the place? I'll keep you working. You can save your money, and then you'll have a chance to put a down payment on an apartment. This could be that new beginning you're looking for."

If you ever wanted a Night Before Christmas story, this was it.

So, I turned the keys over to Tom and Jan, giving them full access to our missionary house on High Street—a small, charming, three bedroom row home on the east side of town. The students on vacation were terrific young adults who had traveled from various parts of the country to give a year of their lives to run programs for our inner-city children's ministry. Their only compensation was room and board and the gratification of making a difference. Those young people sacrificially gave of themselves each day. Happily they had traveled home to be with their families and to get some much-needed rest. Surely, I thought, they would agree with my idea of letting a struggling, homeless couple stay in their home.

All was unfolding according to a good plan. Tom and Jan were grateful to be saving a little money. I was getting work completed. If there was ever a holy hunch, this was it. Our little church was not just giving these folk a handout—we were giving them a hand up, helping them get established and opening a door to a brighter future.

So, at three in the afternoon on Christmas Eve, with a wide smile, I bid my homeless friends a merry Christmas and heartily encouraged them to enjoy a few days of rest . . . with pay. "Have a great Christmas," I said with a wave from the porch. "See you in a few days!"

A Story Not Finished

"Reverend Main?" A gruff voice on the other end of the telephone interrupted my New Year's day, a day set aside to celebrate, sip some eggnog with my wife, and enjoy watching our children play with their new toys.

"Yes, this is Bruce," I replied with curiosity. He didn't sound like one of our parishioners.

"This is Tom," he continued, raising my anxiety. I instinctively sat at attention.

"Do you know the brown Honda Accord at the staff house?" There was a pause. "I borrowed the car, and somebody ran into me as I was coming off the bridge. Don't worry, I'll be able to fix it." Tom went on to tell me that he had been in the auto body business. Within a few days, he assured me, the car would be fixed.

Honda Accord? Julie had just bought an Accord. One of our missionaries. She'd just received some inheritance money and bought a car.

I hung up the phone. All of a sudden Nat King Cole's crooning "O Holy Night" in the background didn't provide the same sense of solace it had a few minutes before. I had a big problem. So much for a Happy New Year.

At that point, getting the car fixed was not my biggest concern. My biggest concern—or should I say embarrassment—was calling the vacationing staff and telling them how I had decided to house a homeless couple in their house, how they had "borrowed" a car, and how they had probably rummaged through their personal belongings. And rummage they had. More than a few things had gone missing.

So were Tom and Jan. Gone. I never saw them again.

Needless to say, the next few days of vacation were not my most memorable. Fortunately the virtues of forgiveness and grace that our missionaries were teaching the children in our programs were also extended to me. Still, I was embarrassed, angry, and out of a bunch of money. I had been duped, and now I was left to untangle the consequences. So much for being the Good Samaritan.

But hadn't I had a hunch? Wasn't it a holy hunch? I was sincerely trying to help some needy folk, trying to live out the implications of the Good Samaritan story. Was I wrong in making the decisions I had made?

Could I have used a little more wisdom in my decision-making process? My critics might tell me that I should not have offered our missionary house to complete strangers—too much temptation for people who had nothing. And perhaps my critics are right. But the problem with hunches is that they often call us to do things and go places that may not make the most rational sense. Obviously, in the parable of the Good Samaritan, there were a few people who thought it not "rational" to stop for a broken man on the side of the road. After all, the road was notorious for robbers and thieves. The wounded man could have been acting and could have been working in collaboration with some friends in hiding. The Samaritan could have been mugged, robbed, or killed. His hunch to help could have turned bad.

And that's the problem with following our hunches. Sometimes they *do* go bad. So the question becomes: how do we deal with hunches that lead us into situations that are not desirable?

Moving Forward

A favorite sermon of mine is called "Shattered Dreams" by Dr. Martin Luther King Jr. Unfortunately, I never heard him preach it. I imagine, however, King's powerful cadences and unique inflections—I would have enjoyed the sermon more than the written text. His intellect, his aptitude to make theological sense out of his social circumstances, and his ability to speak in a language that even the uneducated could understand is unsurpassed.

In "Shattered Dreams" King uses a rather obscure verse from the Epistle to the Romans—"Whensoever I take my journey into Spain, I will come to you" (15:24 KJV)—as his central theme. In all my years of reading the book of Romans, I had never thought to ponder the implications of this buried verse toward the end of the letter.

King reminds the listener that the apostle Paul had a desire to travel to Spain and visit the Christian church in Rome during his pilgrimage. It would be like leaving New York City for Cuba, with a stop in Tampa Bay—quite a trip without a plane, train, or automobile. But Paul, it seems, had a yearning to proclaim the Christian gospel to the outermost fringes of the Roman Empire, considered by many the edge of the earth. I can only guess at the passion, fortitude, and faith to take that kind of trip in that day.

Some might have called Paul's dream foolish. Sure, some people laughed, but deep within Paul's being was this intuitive sense—this hunch—that he needed to go to Spain. Paul, informed by God's spirit and guided by a heart that loved to watch the lives of people be transformed because of his Good News message, proclaimed his intentions to the community of disciples in Rome.

But, interestingly, disappointingly, Paul's hunch was never realized as he intended. King reminds us that "he never got to Rome according to the pattern of his hopes. Because of his daring faith in Jesus Christ, he was indeed taken there, but as a prisoner, and was held captive in a little prison cell. Nor did he ever walk the dusty roads of Spain. . . . Paul's life is a tragic story of a shattered dream."[13] One can only imagine his disappointment and dejection. Paul had a sense to do something for God, and yet his longing was never fulfilled. Paul's faithfulness to share God's Word had gotten him in trouble with the law and reduced him to a prisoner. It was Paul's faithfulness to God, not his disobedience, that inevitably turned a hunch into a tragic disappointment.

So, how does Paul respond to a life event that could have potentially turned him to anger, resentment, and depression? King provides four possible responses and some helpful insights for people whose hunches do not turn out the way they had hoped.

Becoming Bitter and Resentful

The first response is to become bitter and resentful. This is the reaction for many of us, but King contended that the eventual outcome of responding in this way is to "develop a callous attitude, a cold heart, and a bitter hatred toward God, toward those with whom he lives, and toward himself."[14] It is easy to see how this attitude begins, especially for those whose hunches turn in negative directions—like with my homeless people at the church. It would have been easy to internalize my feelings of anger about their lack of responsibility (they had none!). It would have been easy to vent my anger on the next needy person to knock on the church door; it would have been easy to stereotype all homeless people with the same broad strokes and believe that not one was honest. Anger and resentment knock on the door of our heart every time our acts of compassion are exploited and received with ingratitude. The seed of bitterness begins to grow whenever we blame God for not meeting our expectations. For those engaging in a life that responds faithfully to hunches, anger is an occupational hazard that needs to be held at bay.

Withdrawing and Going Inward

The second response, contended King, is to become completely withdrawn and an introvert. Poignantly, King quotes, "Too unconcerned to love and too passionless to hate, too detached to be selfish and too lifeless to be unselfish, too indifferent to experience joy and too cold to experience sorrow, they are neither dead nor alive; they merely exist."[15] How many of us have a tendency to move in this direction when we have been hurt or burned? Rather than getting angry, we just shut ourselves off from the world. Full of justification, we build walls of protection around our hearts, deflecting any future potential of pain and suffering. After eighteen years of working in one of America's neediest cities, I can fully appreciate King's caution. Tom and Jan were not the first to squelch a hunch, nor were they the last. Kids I have helped have burned our buses. Teens I have counseled have stolen from my family. Staff workers with whom I have prayed have spread malicious rumors. Our human response is to withdraw and detach ourselves from the potential of pain. But King reminds us that withdrawal is not a long-term option for a healthy and vibrant faith.

Embracing Fatalism

The third way we respond when things do not go our way is to adopt a fatalistic philosophy toward life. Fatalism implies that everything—all the things that happen to us—are predestined and inescapable. People who embrace this way of thinking believe that human beings have little or no real freedom. As a friend reminds me when we have conversations about the sovereignty of God, "If the deck is rigged, why play the game?" Therefore, he would say, nothing we do really matters. We are merely puppets, and God is the puppeteer. But King contends that fatalism is "based on an appalling conception of God, for everything, whether good or evil, is considered to represent the will of God."[16] Then King goes on to say that a "healthy religion rises above the idea that God wills evil."[17] For those who have been raised in religious traditions that advocate God orchestrating every move of our lives, this brand of coping with disappointment can be very appealing. When our hunches do not unfold as we hope, resorting to "it was God's will" is a kind of escapism that can be tempting to embrace. But King would argue against that kind of coping. He would argue that it is bad theology and would challenge us to rethink our concept of God and how God works in the world. Imagine if King, after being arrested in Birmingham, had announced to the world, "Since we're meeting such opposition, I guess it's God's will that African-Americans live in subordinate roles to whites." Thank goodness King's theology did not allow him to embrace opposition—the fire hoses, the vicious dogs, the lynchings, the death threats on his life, the imprisonments—as "the will of God."

So what do we do? What do we do when we act with the best intentions, when we try to obey hunches that seek to improve the world and the conditions of our brothers and sisters, and then have them backfire and turn into something negative? How are we to respond when the Toms and Jans of the world take our compassionate efforts and carelessly toss them to the wind? King has an answer.

Embracing Our Disappointments

King says we deal with disappointment—or hunches that turn sour—by accepting the "unwanted and unfortunate circumstances even as we cling to a radiant hope."[18]

He goes on to add that it is critical to confront our shattered dreams. We need to place these failures at the forefront of our minds and stare at them and ask, "How may I transform this liability into an asset? How may I, confined in some narrow Roman cell and unable to reach life's Spain, transmute this dungeon of shame into a haven of redemptive suffering."[19] Just like the apostle Paul, who embraces the reality of his jail cell and converts it into a writing studio to pen letters that would guide the church for centuries, we must embrace these potentially discouraging circumstances and allow God to show us how they can be converted into something wonderful.

It is not easy to stare disappointment in the face. We live in a culture that promotes and expects the good life at every turn. Much of our advertising industry is built around making life easier, more convenient, and less painful; don't our pharmaceutical industries provide every imaginable drug for every discomfort? Our society worships leisure and entertainment, providing the ultimate distraction for dealing with our shattered dreams and crushed hopes. Even our Christian faith has been hijacked, heralding Jesus as the ultimate narcotic—"follow Jesus, and life will be filled with blessing, not difficulty." Faithfulness will be rewarded with financial blessing and career success: no hardship, no difficulties. Little is mentioned from pulpits about "death to self," "taking up a cross," or "giving that makes us economically vulnerable." Faith, in the words of Karl Marx, too often has become the opiate of the masses.

But the apostle Paul and Dr. King provided for us an alternative vision for Christian faith. They followed their hunches but found disappointment at every turn, even though they acted in faithfulness. Both were jailed. Both were beaten. Both ridiculed. Both had their lives threatened. Did they become embittered men? Resentful? Did they withdraw and become cloistered monks? Did they just accept their circumstances and abandon their mission? No. Paul at Philippi, incarcerated in a nasty dungeon, hanging on to life by a thread, body beaten, decided to . . . sing songs at midnight. It was Paul who, despite his numerous disappointments, called out, "I have learned in whatsoever state I am, therewith to be content" (Phil. 4:11). King, in a Birmingham jail, scribes his manifesto for the landmark civil rights movement. It is possible to embrace our shattered dreams and allow God to transform them into something beautiful.

Is It Going to Be Intense?

One day I received a phone call from a potential summer intern. Each summer I recruit university-age students from around the world to serve among the poor in the inner city in some of the most difficult circumstances imaginable. Usually the students are motivated by some prompting of the Spirit, responding to something deep within their souls compelling them to act on a fundamental of Christian faith—to serving the poor, showing compassion to the forgotten, and becoming a voice for justice. The students seldom have any idea what they are getting themselves into. It's a leap of faith.

"Is it going to be intense?" asked Phillip, the potential intern on the other end of the phone.

I dodged the question and asked about his present employment. He worked in a Christian coffeehouse in Seattle. "I serve espressos and low-fat cappuccinos to patrons. We play Jars of Clay as background music, no Marvin Gaye or the Rolling Stones. Instead of having copies of the *New York Times* lying around, we have *Christianity Today* and copies of Tim LaHaye's end-time novels."

After proudly describing his resume again he wanted to know, "Is it going to be intense?"

I responded rhetorically. "Ummm . . . well, it depends on what you mean by *intense.*"

"You know, is it going to be difficult?"

"Well, if you call 105-degree days, sharing a shower with 20 other housemates, 6-day work weeks, 12-hour work days, drug dealers hanging on your front porch 'intense,' then I would have to give you a resounding yes. It'll be really intense. Probably the most difficult summer of your life—I'll give you my word on that!"

Silence.

I added, "But I guarantee you that it'll be the best summer of your life. Despite the intensity, God will do things, even some surprising miracles in you and through you, that right now are unimaginable. I hope you decide to come."

Phillip never sent an application. He never made it to the streets of Camden. Could he have settled for serving mochas in Seattle?

For most of our students who follow their hunches and make it to the inner city for a summer, the reality is that they come to a point where their rosy-colored illusions of grand, world-changing service collides with the reality of indifferent violence and gross poverty—that's about the second week. The dream of saving hundreds of children from lives of impoverishment is shattered. At that point they must make a decision: either they embrace their shattered dream or get angry, withdraw, or claim some kind of fatalistic attitude. But for those who grapple with their unfulfilled expectations and disappointments, the opportunities for growth and personal transformation are birthed.

I have learned over the years that following hunches that move us toward acts of compassion, justice, truth, and selfless love is not for the fainthearted. Moving spontaneously and with determination in directions that place us in vulnerable situations is something that can lead to tremendous disappointment and pain. Remember, success is never promised to those who respond to the promptings of God's Spirit in their lives. Look at the lives of the unnumbered Christians of antiquity who responded to their noble hunches, yet in doing so invited great difficulty into their lives. The biblical vision of faith contends that there will be surprising blessings for those who are persecuted, and sometimes death on a cross.

But, be of good cheer, for it is in the midst of our shattered expectations that we get to see a sometimes strange and always wonderful power at work; it'll be a power that takes a cross, an instrument of torture and death, and turns it into the symbol of hope and new life.

CONCLUSION

A QUEST, A HUNCH, UNSPEAKABLE JOY

> So why are Christians so often so joyless? It is, I think,
> because too often Christians have only enough religion
> to make themselves miserable.
>
> William Sloane Coffin

Let me, in this conclusion, introduce my friend Barry.

Barry is a successful businessman who puts together unique and profitable transactions. He describes himself as a fighter—by saying that nothing has ever been given to him. "I've worked for everything." He is known in his industry for shrewd and creative negotiations; some have even described this middle-aged man as intimidating. After all, one does not grow a multimillion-dollar business without conflicts and developing a tough exterior.

He visited me one day at my office. Soon after hellos, his eyes began to redden with tears. I was caught off guard. His display of vulnerability was genuine and real. Here was a local, successful businessman displaying tremendous emotion in my office.

"When my twenty-two-year-old daughter Jen was killed in an auto accident in 1997," he sputtered, "I vowed to get her diploma from the university. She was a senior, just three credits shy of the requirements for graduation, but the school never consented to acknowledge her accomplishments."

Barry had come to visit our ministry and look at our various programs. But he startled me when he started talking about his daughter.

"Can you believe it? Jen only needed three credits to graduate from college when she was killed," he repeated, obviously disappointed by the university bureaucracy and their unwillingness to bend. "And she had a learning difficulty, which made it almost impossible for her to pass the needed math requirement. But she did it. She was even taking a special class at another college." Barry paused and wiped the corner of his eyes. "One June morning she was killed in a car accident on her way home from class."

How might I respond if one of my children were prematurely killed? Even thinking about it makes me shudder. It would gnaw at my being for the rest of my life. The "what ifs" would haunt—"What if we hadn't given her the car that day?" "What if we had gone on a family vacation?" My feelings were true for Barry. Eight years had passed—the pain was still close to the surface. All the financial and professional success in the world could not change things. Jen was gone, and her loss was felt every day.

Barry told me that life had not been easy for Jen. She had been diagnosed with a learning disability. Nobody ever thought she would learn a second language, yet she became proficient in French. Nobody thought she would be able to go to college, let alone graduate, yet she clawed and scratched her way to her senior year at a reputable liberal arts university. One-hundred-and-twenty-six credits completed! Just a few shy of becoming the first in her family to attain a university degree. Barry reminded me that taped to her desk was a poem called "Don't Quit." It was Jen's mantra: "So stick to the fight when you're hardest hit. It's when things seem worst that you musn't quit."

But it was Jen's love for the underdog that impressed everyone.

"She was a fairly quiet kid," added her dad. "But when Jen sensed an injustice, you can bet she asserted herself and spoke up. Her life as the underdog gave her an uncanny ability to feel for and identify with those who were forgotten and mistreated by society."

Barry without pausing told a poignant story about something that happened after his daughter died. Earlier she had attended a large public high school. After Jen died, her former principal called to offer condolences. Barry was amazed that the woman even knew his daughter's name. "I'll always remember Jen," the principal said. "I remember she was the only student who ever interrupted me while I was meeting with my district superintendent. She had to tell me right away about a needy tenth grader." This girl weighed about 350 pounds and had a horrible home life—alcoholic parents, sexual abuse, and despite the affluence of the community, she lived in poverty. She had tried to commit suicide several times. But Jen befriended the girl, brought her home on many occasions, and stuck up for her when other kids ridiculed and teased her.

"The only thing this overweight teen lived for was band," the principal continued. "Band practice and the concerts were the highlight of her life. She just lived to play in the band. Unfortunately and unintentionally, on the day when the band director handed out the uniforms, there was none for her. She was just too big. Kids snickered, since everyone had to have a uniform to play in the band. Consequently, she was asked to leave the band. This did not sit well with Jen. She stormed my office." The principal laughed. "That was my introduction to your daughter. And she wouldn't leave until I made the band teacher take the girl back."

Barry went on to tell me that not only was Jen instrumental in getting this disadvantaged teen back into the band, but she also used her babysitting money to get a custom uniform made for her. That was only part of Jen's legacy. There were more stories, and Jen was the daughter Barry wanted honored.

A Hunch

"I was in the shower this morning," Barry said, "and I had a hunch while shampooing my hair."

His tears had subsided, and he clicked into his businessman mode. He was ready to make a deal. He wanted something and was hoping I would help. "You have connections at my daughter's old university," he continued. "I just had this sense that you might be able to help. I know it's a long shot, but I thought I'd act on a hunch and ask."

We ended our conversation and shook hands. I assured him I would try but could not guarantee anything. I would call and see if the president could help even though I knew there were policies and committees that made these decisions; there were regulations and expectations to maintain institutional accreditation. If the family had been denied the posthumous degree by the university, why would they grant it this time?

The Visit

My meeting with the new university president the next week went extremely well. He assured me that he would look into the situation, and I left his office hopeful. (Especially since Christmas was just around the corner, I thought maybe, just maybe. What better gift for the family?)

Two weeks later and four days before the winter graduation ceremony, I received the news. The university would honor Jen with a Bachelor of Science degree. Not only that, but there would be four VIP tickets for the family, a private lunch with the school president, and the honor for Barry to receive the diploma on his daughter's behalf. A father's quest had been fulfilled.

The Letter

The week after the graduation I received this note from Barry:

I am amazed at the intervention of time, events, and people in our lives. How a teacher, a neighbor, or friend can influence our path! All credit to God and the Holy Spirit who charts our walk, our conduct.

While in the shower daydreaming one morning, you and the university came to mind. Now how did that thought occur? It had to be of God! As you know of my Jen's story, unfinished business weighed on my heart. . . .

On Saturday Jean and I joyfully accepted Jen's degree in Business Administration. We were so moved and grateful. My family was there to see the whole godly ceremony. Certainly a marker in our lives. I was personally moved, overwhelmed. Emotion that had built up over the last eight years poured out of me, I guess. We felt a great sense of accomplishment about what Jen earned and deserved.

Not every hunch, as we have discussed in this book, ends so wonderfully. But it is evident that acting on our hunches can be the beginning of a chain of events that give God's spirit an opportunity to move in miraculous and wonderful ways.

As in Barry's case, his willingness to act on a hunch led to closure and a time to diffuse some feelings toward an institution with which he had some unfinished business. If Barry had not acted, nothing would have happened.

Certainly Barry had all the justification in the world *not* to act. How easy it would have been to say, "My efforts didn't work in the past; why bother now?" But Barry followed an inkling, an intuition, a hunch, and that intuitive sense that the Spirit was moving. And because of his love for his daughter and his commitment to seeing justice for all her hard work, he acted.

That morning when Barry voiced his hunch, he joined a lineage of people throughout history who stepped out in faith and opened channels for God to move. Just like the religious leader who followed his hunch, believing that Jesus would somehow heal his daughter, or the four friends who carried their paralytic friend across town to encounter the teacher-healer, or the bleeding woman who risked it all when she thought Jesus might be able to do something no other doctor could do, Barry, too, followed his hunch . . . with the expectation that God might do something extraordinary.

This is the tradition we are asked to join.

A life that grows in faith and is open to the prompting of God's Spirit is a life that will receive hunches. A life that responds faithfully to those hunches will be a life full of challenges and opportunities to watch God work in some extraordinary and unique, creative ways.

May you step forward today with discerning spontaneity, living as a conduit of God's lavish love and bountiful grace.

NOTES

1. The story of Daryl and Darrel made our local newspaper in an article entitled "A Long-Distance Education: Professors Travel 850 Miles to Teach Camden Class." Luis Puga, *Courier Post*, June 7, 2004, 2B.

2. Many people assume that St. Francis actually penned this prayer. It is doubtful. Most scholars feel it was first composed at a Catholic eucharistic congress in Chicago in 1925. Without a doubt it captures the theme of Francis's life. I need to add that the reporter did not recite the whole prayer, only a portion. I included the whole prayer in the account of the story because of its poignancy as a complete literary piece.

3. James W. Fowler, *Weaving the New Creation: Stages of Faith and the Public Church* (San Francisco: HarperSanFrancisco, 1991), 38.

4. Ibid., 38.

5. Marianne Williamson, *Return to Love* (New York: HarperPerennial, 1992), 190–91. Many people have attributed these words directly to Mandela. Closer research reveals that they were written by Williamson and, perhaps, used by Mandela in one of his speeches.

6. C. S. Lewis, *Mere Christianity* (New York: Collier Books, 1960), 109.

7. Gordon Atkinson, "Following Red," *The Christian Century*, December 14, 2004, 9.

8. William Sloane Coffin, *Credo* (Louisville: Westminster John Knox Press, 2004), 7.

9. *The Wittenburg Door*, January/February 2005, 13. An interview with Peggy Wehmeyer, religion correspondent for ABC News, on World Vision Radio. This was one of Mike Yaconelli's last interviews before he tragically died. In the interview they talk a lot about a Youth Specialties/World Vision project called One Life Revolution, a program that seeks to provide help in AIDS-ridden Zambia.

10. Ibid., 14.

11. Oscar Romero, *The Violence of Love* (Farmington, PA: The Plough Publishing House, 1998), 139.

12. Ibid., 127.
13. Martin Luther King Jr., *Strength to Love* (Glasgow: Collins, 1963), 86.
14. Ibid., 88.
15. Ibid.
16. Ibid.
17. Ibid.
18. Ibid.
19. Ibid.

⇧ NOTES

Bruce Main is a graduate of Fuller Seminary, with his DMin from Princeton. He is the executive director of UrbanPromise Ministries in Camden, New Jersey, and has developed satellite programs in several other cities (www.urbanpromise usa.org). He is an international conference speaker and the coauthor of several books, including *Spotting the Sacred*.

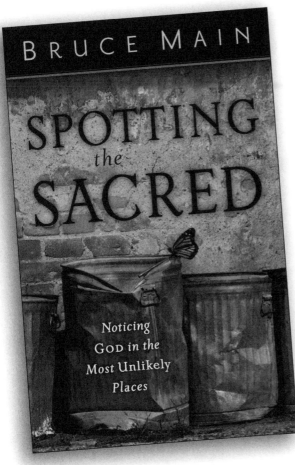